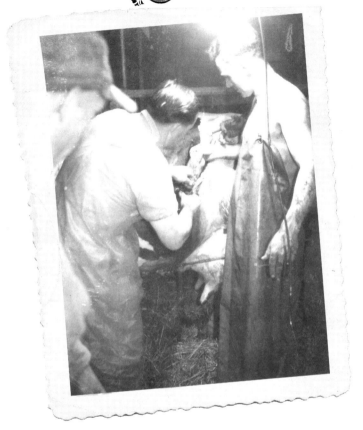

# MUD, SWEAT
# AND TEARS

Previous page: Bud Ings (left) and Bob Webster, student vet (right), perform a caesarian section on a cow, 1957

# MUD, SWEAT AND TEARS
## Tales of a Country Vet

### Bud Ings

The Acorn Press
Charlottetown
2008

Mud, Sweat and Tears © 2008 by Bud Ings
ISBN 1-894838-38-6      978-1-894838-38-2

Editing by Marian Bruce
Design by Matthew MacKay
Printing in Canada by Hignell Book Printing

The author acknowledges the support of the Prince Edward Island Council of the Arts which provided a creation grant for the writing of this book.

The publisher acknowledges the support of the Government of Canada through the Book Publishing Industry Development Program (BPIDP) of the Department of Canadian Heritage for our publishing activities. We also acknowledge the support of the Canada Council for the Arts and the Prince Edward Island Department of Communities, Cultural Affairs, and Labour for our publishing program.

Library and Archives Canada Cataloguing in Publication

Ings, Bud, 1926-
        Mud, sweat, and tears / Bud Ings.

ISBN 978-1-894838-38-2

        1. Ings, Bud, 1926-. 2. Veterinarians—Anecdotes.
3. Veterinarians—Prince Edward Island—Biographies.
I. Title.

SF613.I54A3 2008      636.089092      C2008-906101-2

ACORNPRESS

P.O. Box 22024
Charlottetown, Prince Edward Island
C1A 9J2
acornpresscanada.com

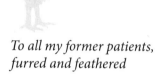

*To all my former patients,*
*furred and feathered*

# Contents

Bud Ings in Guelph, 1950

# Acknowledgements

Thanking all the people who helped me along the way is somewhat risky, as there is always a danger of forgetting someone. There were many who encouraged me to write these stories.

I was first inspired to put my experiences as a country veterinarian on paper by James Herriot's wonderful series. He had it even tougher than I did.

I am grateful to the many friends and farmers who reminded me of things that happened when I was treating or saving an animal patient.

I was fortunate to have many summer students working with me over the years. The vet students became part of the family during the summer, and learning became a two-way street! I was kept up-to-date on new procedures, while I showed them the practice side of veterinary life. Most became lifelong friends and continue to keep in touch. I want to thank the long list of great vet students for their help and enthusiasm during the days of red mud and sweat.

My wife, Connie, who attended to the office and answered the phone all through the years — in addition to answering the doorbell hundreds of times, dispensing drugs, and, most important, paying the bills — had to be the most important member of the team, which included my three daughters, Jeanne, Joanne, and Jayne. Every story began with a telephone call when a member of my family answered the phone and relayed the message of an animal in need of care.

I would also like to thank the Prince Edward Island Council of the Arts for its support.

And, last but not least, thanks to my editor and friend Marian Bruce, for her encouragement, support, and expertise.

*May 21, 1952*

# Students Will Get Degree In Veterinary Medicine

The Senate of the University of Toronto announces that the following candidates obtained the standing indicated at the final examination for the degree of Doctor of Veterinary Medicine held recently at the Ontario Veterinary College.

The Degree of Doctor of Veterinary Medicine will be conferred upon the successful candidates at a special convocation of the University to be held in the Memorial Hall of the Ontario Agricultural College, Guelph, at 11.15 a.m. Tuesday, May 20, 1952.

**Honors 1** — Ainslie, K. R., Benjamin, N. H., Calverley, A. H., Calverley, B. J. (Mrs.), Campbell, E. B., Corner, A. H., Fleming, G. C., Frederick, G. L., Glenney, L. E., Graham, R. T. A., Guilbert, H. L., Harold, D. S., Hodgson, J. A., Humble, R. J. Ingram, D. G., Julian, R. J., Kirby, I. A. E., Leitch, G. L., Maude, A. E., North, E. B., Rossoni, L. J., Sheehy, G. E., Stephen, L. E., Stratas, W. J., Thomas, L. A., Willigan, D. A.

**Honors 11** — Addison, A. W., Alexander, D. C., Atrill, M. E., Bissonnette, P. H. H., Boisclair, R. W. E., Brown, N. M., Burch, W. L., Cahill, W. K., Cawley, A. J., Clark, M. H., Clerke, A. S., Cooper, E. L., Doidge, G. R., Donovan, L. A., DuPlessis, D. M., Fish, R. D., Furness, T. R., Graham, K. D., Hackney, J. C., Hamilton, G. F., Hardy, P. Y. D. (Mrs.), Hess, G. J., Hulet, J. G., Ings, A. E., Jelly, G. G., Johnson, J. V., Jones, H. W., Jablonski, Z., Kelly, H. H., Laursen, A. C., Lawreniuk, W., Ludolph, W. C., Mitchell, L. E., Mitton, A. R., Morelli, E. J. E., MacLennan, D. C., MacNeill, A. C., McKay, G. W., McKersie, W. K., McKibbin, L. S., McLaurin, D. E., McWatt, E. M., Neily, L. G., Packham, J. W., Price, D. J., Roenisch, H. W., Smith, J. D., Spracklin, R. W., Stovell, P. L., Treleaven, D. C., Trenholm, K. W., Trout, K. J., Vidugiris, B., Walker, F. W., Webster, D. E. J. (Miss) Whitehead, J. R., Wood, M. E. (Miss), Woodstock, J. J., Wright, T. T., Zlotnick, H.

**Pass Standing** — Badame, F. G., Dingwall, W. J., Gulyas, F. A.

Newspaper article announcing Bud's graduation, May 21, 1952

# 1

## Bessie and the Young Vet

It was one of those baffling cases they don't tell you about in veterinary school: a Holstein cow that simply refused to get up. As I knelt by the motionless animal sprawled in the stall, the owner, a gruff old farmer with fifty years' experience with livestock, stared at me with one eye closed. "Me dad would have me cow on her feet if he was alive," he said in a booming voice. "Two things me dad always did for downed cows. Pour water in their ears and cut a piece off their tails to let the poison out. You never did that."

True, I had not tried either remedy.

I was an inexperienced veterinarian, less than a year out of vet school, and still trying to prove myself. The patient was a black-and-white cow named Bessie, and she was lying on her side in a stable in northeastern Prince Edward Island, apparently almost unconscious. Her owner, Pius MacDonald, was becoming impatient. He was not the kind of person who would wait long for results, and from the start I could tell that he was not impressed with me. No wonder. I was in my mid-twenties, slight and boyish-looking. Moreover, unlike the local amateur vets he was used to dealing with, I was a college graduate — grounds for suspicion right there — and came from a community thirty miles away. He had never heard of me.

To me, Bessie's problem looked like a classic case of "milk fever," an illness that sometimes afflicts high-pro-

Bud's graduation photo from the Ontario
Veterinary College, 1952

ducing dairy cows after calving. The name of the ailment
is misleading. The animal doesn't really have a fever, but,
in many cases, it has a below-normal temperature due to
a sudden loss of calcium in the blood. If the cow is not
treated quickly, she probably will die. On my first visit, I
injected the standard dose of calcium and waited for the
best part of an hour for Bessie to rise. No results. Finally
I told the owner that, if she was still not on her feet by
morning, he should call me.

Sure enough, the call came the next morning. Bessie
was still down. Would I please come and see what I could
do? At vet school, I had been told that one of the cases that
could really get under a vet's skin was a cow that refused

to get up. It was as hard to diagnose as a mysterious itch. Apparently, my day had arrived. Worse, I knew it would be difficult for a young doctor to convince a seasoned farmer like this one that any number of problems might be to blame.

In the course of four visits to the farm, I tried everything I could think of that would stimulate that black-and-white beast. Nothing worked. I was beginning to think that Bessie was enjoying the whole thing. She was eating like a horse and seemed pleased with all the attention she was getting. But she would not attempt to move.

On my fifth visit, I was greeted by five or six experts from neighbouring farms. Each of the animal specialists had his own unique opinion. One remedy that was "never known to fail" involved sprinkling a downed cow with Holy Water from the church.

After a half-hour of these consultations, I thought I heard a snap in Bessie's pelvic region. I decided to do a rectal examination, and asked my consultants to move the cow back and forth. Sure enough, there was movement in the pelvis that indicated a fracture. Finally, I had uncovered the reason for Bessie's immobility. "Your cow has a broken pelvis, Mr. MacDonald," I announced, "and she'll never get to her feet."

I felt as though I were in front of a firing squad. Mr. MacDonald raised a finger and boomed, "I just wish me dad was alive. A smart man, he was. He'd have that cow back in the pasture by now. You can't get the old bugger up, but he could have."

"I'm sorry, sir," I said, "but you might as well call the packers. I can't do anything more for your cow." I could see the disappointment in the old man's eyes. As I turned to go, he shouted, "You never even got me dog to bark at her head!"

I thought perhaps there would be no harm in the dog therapy, and, to please everyone present, I invited the resi-

Bud's grandfather Albert Ings (left) and Bud (right), 1944

Grandpa and I were running short of individual lambing pens, which we erected on the spot to give the new mothers breathing space and the newborns a measure of protection. One of the most important practices at lambing time is to make sure that the new arrivals get a suck of colostrum, the first milk that contains the life-protecting elements to protect lambs from disease and infection. That evening, a lot of lamb-like sounds started all around the sheep barn, adding to the confusion. Hidden by the darkness, I was moving quickly from one place to another, crying out like my fleecy charges. Frustrated, Grandpa finally called out: "Get to the house and get your father. There's damn lambs all over the place, and I can't find them!"

In addition to the livestock, our farm was also home to a variety of dogs and cats, each with a distinct personality. One dog I was particularly close to was Gimmy, a big red cross between a Collie and a Great Dane. One winter, Father built a big sled for the monstrous dog to haul. If grain for the cattle happened to be in short supply, Dad would dispatch Gimmy and me to go to the mill for a bag of dairy feed. That was faster and more convenient than hitching a horse. It was nothing for Gimmy to haul two bags at a time.

But Gimmy's real talent — or, at least, his passion — was rounding up the cows. Unfortunately, his imposing presence and somewhat aggressive style — somewhat like a dyspeptic sergeant-major in the armed forces — meant we had to keep him on a leash. His very presence terrified the cows. If Gimmy had the milk cows running, and he was within range of Grandpa's failing vision, there was big trouble for the dog and me when we got to the stable. "You'll have all my cows dry, hurrying them along like that," Grandpa would mutter. "Leave that darn dog in the barn!" Knowing that he was out of favour, Gimmy would head for the dark turnip cellar, where Grandpa was unlikely to spot him.

On other occasions, though, Grandpa called on Gimmy's services. Twice a day, a steam-driven Canadian National Railways train roared through the middle of our farm, on its run between Charlottetown and Murray Harbour. There was a barricade between our fields and the tracks, but occasionally one of our cattle, terrified by the commotion, broke through the fence. Gimmy always obligingly brought the stray back to the farm. "My, what a great dog you are!" Grandpa would say, no doubt confusing the poor fellow.

When his cattle-herding duties slowed down, Gimmy started setting his sights on another challenge — the train itself. One day, out of the clear blue sky, he decided to chase the iron menace off the farm. Not only was the train exceptionally noisy; it also rumbled through our

Earl Ings and Virginia the mare, 1942

fields a little too fast, even for Gimmy. For at least a year, Gimmy chased the train every day. Then, he apparently decided that the train travelled more slowly going east to Murray Harbour in the afternoon than on the morning run to Charlottetown. One afternoon as the train was going past the barn, Gimmy caught up with the last passenger train, grabbed the rubber hose coupling, bit a hole in it and promptly stopped the train. As the air escaped, the train came to a squealing halt. All hell broke loose. The conductor and engineer came running, shouting and shaking their fists at the big red dog. Gimmy, realizing that he was in trouble again, high-tailed it to the cow barn. I headed for the barn with him. In the safety of his hiding place, a look of satisfaction was written all over that dog's face. There was no need to talk. We understood each other perfectly.

Another animal that made a big impression on me was Virginia, the sleek standardbred racing mare that took me to school in Charlottetown one year. In retrospect, those trips were probably good training for the years I would spend on the road as a veterinarian.

In the early years of the Second World War, I went to

the local two-room school. But when I was in Grade 10, the teacher quit at Christmas, and there was little chance of finding a substitute, as young men and women were joining the armed services at a great rate. My parents decided to send me to West Kent School in Charlottetown.

The city school was only six miles from our farm, but in those days, that was a long distance. Cars, trucks, and tractors were rare, and most roads were unpaved and often blocked with snow in winter. My father always kept a driving horse or "blood" horse in addition to the strong but slow draft horses. Virginia, our standardbred mare, was fast, but she was also very nervous.

Virginia was afraid of just about everything, but especially of automobiles, and particularly if their window wipers were in motion. I had to travel across the Hillsborough Bridge and down the main street of Charlottetown, and when I met a motor vehicle, Virginia always tried to turn around and run away. If we met a bus on the bridge, and the windshield wipers were running, I had to get out of the sleigh or sulky and lead her past those frightening creatures. One day one of the bus drivers turned off his wipers and shouted, "You should put a bag over her head, lad! And some wax in her ears so she won't hear the motor!"

During the spring, after a heavy, soft snowfall, the going was tough. I used a speed sleigh with a body about two feet off the road, but the tracking was deep, and often the sleigh got stuck. Then I had to jump out to lift the sleigh loose while trying to control the lunging mare. A couple of times, Virginia even broke the traces and walked out of the shafts. Using a lesson learned from my grandfather, I repaired the sleigh using "hay wire" — wire that was used before the days of baling twine to tie bales of hay.

Despite my difficulties with Virginia, she and I became close during those trips to school. At home, I was used to hearing about losses of good cattle and horses for want of professional medical aid. There was only one veterinarian

From left: Anna, Miriam, Eileen, Lillian, Doris, Harley, and Bud in his OVC jacket, July 1951

we could call on in those days, and the man was rushed off his feet, so he was often not available. I was especially worried about Virginia, and wondered what would happen to her if she became ill or got hurt. That spring, Virginia was often up to her knees in mud as she hauled me to town, and I wished I knew more about looking after her many aches and pains. As the eldest son in our family, I was in line to take over the farm. But I was torn. During those long drives with Virginia, I began thinking about another possibility for my future.

In June, hoping to advance to the next level in my education, Prince of Wales College in Charlottetown, I wrote the entrance exams to the college, knowing I didn't have much chance of passing them because I had missed so much of the course work. But a miracle took place: I passed by one mark. When I saw the results in the morning newspaper, I went out to the stable, hugged Virginia for a job well done, and gave her another scoop of grain as a thank you.

My decision had been made: I would study for three years at Prince of Wales, and if my luck held out, and I could scrape up enough money, I would apply to the veterinary school in Ontario.

# 3

## Becoming a Vet

In the fall of 1948, I boarded a train in Charlottetown, paid the conductor twenty-five cents for a pillow and began a two-day journey to Guelph, Ontario, to begin my studies at the Ontario Veterinary College. After sitting up all night because I couldn't afford a $10 berth, I arrived late the next night at the college and settled into a student residence.

That was the beginning of a four-year adventure in education that transformed me from farmer to veterinarian. From today's perspective, the costs of that education seem small — $100 for tuition and $9 a week for room and board — but I was paying my way with the meagre funds we could scrape up from the farm and whatever I could manage to earn by working part-time at the college. Student aid was non-existent. And I knew the next four years were going to be difficult.

My first class at the college did nothing to allay any anxieties. "Look to the left of you," the professor boomed, "and look to the right of you. Because this time next year, one of you will not be here. We will weed you out like carrots!"

As it turned out, that was not an idle threat. Vet colleges across Canada had expanded their classes considerably after the Second World War in an effort to alleviate a chronic shortage of veterinarians, so it was relatively easy to get admitted. The hard part was graduating: it was not unusual for half the class to fail.

Ontario Veterinary College, Guelph, ON, circa 1948

Somehow, I survived, as did two other Island boys who had enrolled at the college at the same time as I did. We had no illusions about getting rich in our chosen careers. Under a provincial veterinary assistance program set up in 1950 on the Island, a veterinarian would be paid $3,000 a year. Farmers paid $3 a call, plus the cost of drugs and surgical procedures. Castrating pigs and bulls, for instance, was a 50¢ job. We knew what we were in for: we'd spend our careers travelling tens of thousands of miles, mostly on clay roads, and we'd be on call twenty-four hours a day, seven days a week. No overtime pay for us.

We would have to rely heavily on the experience we had gained back on the farm, on our own intuition and sometimes on help from above. We would have no X-ray machines for diagnoses; nobody had heard of ultrasound; most surgeries would be conducted in drafty, dirty barns instead of in sterile operating rooms. We were armed with the latest medications: sulfamethazine for pneumonia and other infections (penicillin had just come on the market but, at $10 a shot, was considered very expensive); Epsom salts for anything from bathing cows' udders to constipation; mineral oil for indigestion, colic, and impaction; turpentine for colic; and a calcium preparation, which we would mix ourselves, for milk fevers.

Connie and Jeanne Ings in Guelph, 1952

Fortunately, we were young and idealistic and, in some cases, somewhat obsessed with the idea of providing professional veterinary services.

At the end of my graduation year, I bought a car through a finance company, paying seventeen-per-cent interest (apparently the banks weren't impressed by a doctor of veterinary medicine degree), to drive my bride, Connie, our baby, Jeannie, and me back to the Island. To transport our possessions, I had a trailer made from the remains of an old mobile home and covered everything up with a piece of canvas donated by a friend.

On the way home, we drove through the United States; the Canadian roads were rough, and the TransCanada Highway was just a dream. At the end of our 1,500-mile journey, we boarded the ferry at Cape Tormentine, New Brunswick, delighted that we would soon be back on our good old red soil. As we drove from Borden toward home,

Bud and Jeanne Ings in Guelph, 1951

I remarked to Connie that the Canadian customs officers hadn't bothered to look under the canvas on the trailer to see what we were carrying. "Guess they thought we looked too honest," Connie replied.

Our luck didn't hold out, however. Closer to home, we saw red lights flashing ahead of us, and two Mounties waved us down. "We are looking for moonshine, Sir," one of them said. "We want to search your trailer." The officers, having found only a few suitcases and boxes, soon waved us on our way. "I guess we're really back in PEI, the land of honey and moonshine," I said to Connie. "We're really back home!"

We were home, indeed, but, oddly enough, our destination on the Island was strange territory to both of us. I had been raised near Charlottetown and Connie, in Georgetown, on the southeastern coast of the Island. We were setting up a large-animal practice in Souris, a seaport in northeastern Prince Edward Island. At the time, the Island was divided into five veterinary territories, with clinics in Souris, Montague, Kensington, O'Leary, and Charlottetown. In those days, when cars were few and roads were poor, people needed a good reason to travel far from their home communities. Neither of us had ever been to Souris.

That meant I would be a stranger to farmers whose trust I needed to win. They were used to dealing with people they knew — neighbours with a reputation for curing sick and injured animals. I was an untried young pup.

# 4

## The Trial

**M**y brand-new veterinary practice was less than an hour old when the phone call came. "We have a cow trying to give birth, and we can't get the calf," the caller hollered down the phone line. "Could you come and help us?"

The year was 1952. Connie and I had just arrived at our new home in Souris. Dr. George Fisher, Director of Veterinary Services for the province, showed us to our new apartment, introduced us to the landlord, wished us good luck, and left for Charlottetown. We were on our own. And before we had a chance to unpack our bags, we had our first client.

I told the anxious farmer that we had just arrived in town, and my equipment was still in boxes. "Never mind the equipment, Doc," he said. "We have plenty of rope. We're fishermen, and there's 100 fathoms of line here. All we need is you."

When I hung up, I searched through the newly arrived boxes of supplies and managed to find obstetrical equipment. There was a good chance that the poor animal had been in labour for a long time, so I needed to take some lubrication along as well.

The call had come from the Robertson farm in Kingsboro, about 10 miles east of Souris. It was a large, farming/fishing operation that looked as though it was well-managed. When I pulled up to the main barn, I saw seven or eight husky men standing around, waiting to see the wonder boy deliver the new calf.

"My God," the senior Mr. Robertson said, "are you the vet?"

"Yes," I answered.

"I asked for a man, not a boy, to help in this case," the farmer protested. ""You don't come from these parts, do ya?"

"No," I replied. "I come from a place just east of Charlottetown."

"Yeah, I thought you was a foreigner," the old man said. "We all had a crack at trying to get that calf. We didn't think there was much anyone could do, so we figured we'd try the new vet that was moving into town."

By then, the situation was becoming clear. The cow had been in labour all day, and a small army of locals had worked for several hours without success. Now it was time to see what the new, green vet could do — if anything. I knew that these local midwives were sure the new, green vet would fail. In fact, I could sense that they were hoping I would.

At veterinary school, I had seen very few maternity cases, as most were looked after by veterinarians in the area. But, having been brought up on a large dairy farm, I had assisted in a good number of deliveries. I called on my farm experience and hoped for the best.

Working the lubricating solution into the uterus of the cow, I found a severe deviation of the calf-head. I corrected the birth alignment, placed my calving chains on the forelegs, and silently prayed to God for a miracle. Sure enough, it happened. "Pull hard!" I yelled.

And there was the calf! Oddly, the spectators to this miracle birth showed few signs of rejoicing. Instead, they filed out of the barn looking bewildered and, in some cases, dejected.

On the other hand, I was elated, for a couple of reasons. A new baby had arrived in the world, safe and sound. And I knew that news of this success would spread in the community and give a boost to my new career. I had just earned a little respect from the farmers and fishermen, and from my competition, the local "handymen" — known in some circles as "the quacks."

# 5

## I'm Your Handyman

Connie and I were sleeping peacefully one night when we woke up with a start: a man was standing — and swaying slightly — at the foot of the bed. "Me next-door gentleman and I came by to get your advice on this bad colic," he explained. "We've been slapping him with Dr. Bell's Wonder bottle with poor results, so we thought we better come see the expert."

I recognized the visitor at once. It was one of the neighbourhood "handymen," and he obviously had been sampling from a bottle of another kind. "Would you wait outside until I get dressed?" I shouted. Connie grabbed her housecoat and threatened to get the broom, but fortunately our visitor staggered out of the bedroom without further encouragement, and I followed him to the farm, where a big black Clydesdale horse had been suffering from colic all evening. In spite of the annoyance of being so rudely awakened, I was glad to oblige.

One of the first things a new veterinarian had to learn in the mid-1900s was to gain the confidence of the local "handymen" — men with little formal training but some skill in caring for sick or injured animals. Some folks referred to them as "quacks," but the shortage of qualified animal doctors in the first half of the century meant that farmers learned to rely on the handymen, and there usually was one in each farm community.

Some of these so-called veterinarians took correspondence courses from schools in Michigan, Massachusetts, or Ontario. For a few dollars, you could obtain a certificate in almost any specialty. In the 1950s, I saw a number of equine dentistry diplomas hanging on kitchen walls in King's County. Many of the handymen relied on cures passed down through generations. They obtained medicinal ingredients by mail order, local general stores, or in kitchen cupboards. Mineral oil, ginger, and turpentine were standard remedies. A popular line of cures was marketed under the name "Dr. Bell's Wonder Drugs." One of these "wonder drugs," "Bell's Black Bottle," was touted as a cure-all for everything from diarrhea to constipation. Results were questionable, but in an emergency something had to be done. For their services, some of the "vets" received cash, but sometimes the payment was a meal, a bag of farm produce, the loan of farm equipment, or a promise to help with chores.

I managed to develop a good relationship with a number of the handymen. I often left bits of medicine with them for emergency use, telling them that those new drugs worked faster and better than some of the old home remedies. Sometimes, realizing how little they really knew about medicine, they would hesitate to tackle a difficult case and would call on me instead. Gradually some of them became fast friends. Sometimes the handymen would drop by the clinic to brush up on their skills as vet assistants. Normally I was happy to oblige, although I was somewhat taken aback by a few such visits, as was Connie.

One day when I was on a farm call at noontime, Connie heard a great commotion — squealing and yelling — at the door of the clinic, then located at one end of our house. It was one of my handymen friends, lugging an eighty-pound pig with a hernia, or umbilical rupture, the size of a grapefruit. The pig was covered in excrement and stank to high heaven.

Umbilical and scrotal hernias are a fairly common inherited condition that should be dealt with when the animal is small, perhaps twenty-five pounds or less. Repairs to large hernias are known to break down, and I seldom operated on big pigs with big hernias. When I did operate, I usually performed the procedure in the garage, and because I was on the road so much, the client had to make an appointment.

"What in the world are you doing, coming here with that monstrous pig, and without an appointment?" Connie asked the visitor. "You know better than that."

"Well I figured that he'd get over it faster doing him a bit older," the man replied.

Not knowing what else to do, Connie instructed him to take the pig to the basement and lock him up in the dog kennel. "I don't know when Bud will get back," she said.

When I returned, I did operate, reluctantly, but by that time, the stink had crept into every corner of our house. Connie was not amused. I never did find out how that big pig fared after his operation, but I was fairly confident about one thing: the man who brought him to the house did know better, as Connie had pointed out. I was pretty sure he was testing the new young college grad.

Eighty-pound pigs and night visitors aside, my relationship with the old-time "vets" remained friendly. I helped them, but they also helped me by smoothing my introduction to the farm community. In many cases, the older farmers would call the well-known handyman first. The handymen gradually began referring the difficult cases to me. In any case, by the time I began practising, the era of the "quack" was almost over. The vet colleges were turning out more and more qualified practitioners, and young farmers, in particular, tended to lean toward the university graduates. As agriculture on the Island modernized, many farmers became reluctant to place valuable livestock in the hands of the "quacks." Besides, dealing with the handymen generally took up too much of a farmer's time. He'd usually have to go after the local "vet," give him a meal or two, and drive him home. Using a professional, the farmer only had to make a phone call. And call they did. As the years went by, I became quite used to being called at all hours of the day or night, and to being awakened from a sound sleep — although never again by a man emitting alcohol fumes from the foot of my bed.

# 6

## Baptism by Snow

Only a few months after I graduated from veterinary school, I found out what it was like to attend to my practice in winter. In those days, my caseload, like that of most veterinarians, consisted mostly of farm animals. That meant that I had to be on the road day and night, summer and winter. And for some reason, the most urgent calls seemed to come late at night, and often in the midst of a blizzard or during the Island's infamous mud season.

In those days, the Island had only about 150 miles of pavement. The main paved highway was usually passable — if barely — in winter, but some of the narrow secondary roads remained closed for most of the winter and spring. Heavy snowfalls often made it impossible to plow open even a single track, especially in Prince and King's counties, where the few plows were small and underpowered. To open a road after a big storm, the big "Walters" plows sometimes had to be brought out from the government garage in Charlottetown, as well as caterpillar bulldozers to push the mounds of snow away from the plow. After several snowfalls, the cuttings made by plows often were fifteen or twenty feet high, sometimes even touching the telephone lines.

When the side-roads were closed, I would drive by car as far as possible, often following one of the ever-helpful snowplow operators. At the point where the road became impassible by car, a farmer would meet us with a horse

Clearing the snow in New Perth, 1957

and sleigh and take us the rest of the way, sometimes travelling through the fields, where the snow was not so deep. Climbing in the sleigh, I fervently hoped that I was carrying all the equipment and medicines I would need. Otherwise it would mean a trip back to the car. The snowplow crew would holler out the window, "We'll wait here until you get back. We'll see that you get home okay."

When I had to drive in bad weather, which was often, I kept in touch with the plow dispatcher, who worked hand-in-hand with the plow operator, the farmer, and the doctor, and handled all emergencies — a person needing medical attention, a power outage or a sick animal — with great efficiency.

At noon on one stormy day, I got a call from John MacDonald, a dairy farmer in Mount Stewart, a village about thirty miles away. "I gotta get you down here," the farmer said. "My best cow is trying to calve, and it looks like the calf is too big. All the neighbours were here helping the best they could, but it looks like you may have to operate on her." I had the feeling this man was probably right. But why did it have to storm when calls came in from so far away?

Glancing out the window, I could see that a major winter storm was brewing. "I'll try to see how the travelling is, John," I said, "but the snow is getting thick up here, and the winds are blowing much stronger now. I'll phone the dispatcher, and we'll see how the travelling is." There was a long silence on the other end of the line. I could tell John was worried. "I'll keep in touch with your local telephone operator," I told him. "We'll keep you posted on our progress."

The plow dispatcher arranged for a plow to go as far as the village of Morell on the north side of the Island. A machine from Mount Stewart would meet us for the remainder of the trip. As we ventured across the bridge from the town of Souris, the storm started bearing down on us. I was driving about fifty feet behind the plow, but there were times when I couldn't even see the machine. Snow was piling up on the windshield, making visibility difficult. The car radio reported that the temperature was creeping below minus twenty, and the Mounties were advising people to get off the roads and stay off.

Suddenly I saw the plow leaving the road. The operator, Joe Cheverie, had been unable to see where he was driving at times, and had slipped into the ditch. His plow had no two-way radio, but we had stopped close to a farm home, and Joe managed to find his way to the door to phone the dispatcher. Another plow was only two miles away, and the telephone operator was able to track him down.

"What luck!" Joe said when he came back to the car. "We should get a tow in about twenty minutes. The plow from Dundas is on its way. He was going home after getting the doctor for a sick baby."

Although it seemed as though we were waiting an

hour or more, the big Walters plow, the only one of its kind in that end of the Island, arrived twenty minutes later. When we arrived at Morell, I filled my gas tank — by then showing only one-quarter full. The Dundas plow operator offered to escort me the rest of the way to the MacDonald farm.

At the farm, I found a lovely Holstein cow in the stable, trying to calve but in bad shape. She was cast on her side, quite bloated, and suffering from milk fever, a condition caused by a calcium deficiency that can lead to total collapse and death. "Let's get her propped up, boys," I said. "We haven't much time." Once she was propped up, the gas in her rumen, or stomach, escaped and she belched like a broken balloon. Then I injected calcium, the life-saving antidote, into her jugular vein. The solution trickled slowly through her system, and soon she was back on her feet.

John was all smiles as I pulled on my shoulder-length rubber gloves and prepared to remove the calf — a procedure that was easier to carry out on a cow in the vertical position. I found that the head of the calf had twisted sideways — a condition technically known as lateral deviation. Because of this, it would not be possible to pull the calf out the way the local folks had tried to do. "We have to push the little fellow back into the cow to unlock the calf's head and neck," I said. "We've got to straighten him out."

The head was quite large, indicating that the calf might be a male. Hard as I tried, there was no moving him backward. I would have to inject an anesthetic into the cow's spinal cord to stop her from straining, and would have to judge the amount carefully: too much, and she could topple over and make things worse. Using an average dose, I slowly injected the medication into the cow, hoping for the best. The effect was similar to freezing a tooth. In no time, she relaxed, and I applied a head snare to the infant, being carefully not to choke him. In a few minutes, we delivered a new bull calf to join the rest of the MacDonald herd.

"The Lord be praised!" said John.

"It's wonderful what He can do with such a team of good disciples," I replied.

The new mother began licking her offspring vigorously. For a few minutes, we forgot all about the storm. The feeling of contentment in the stable, with all the cows either eating a meal of fresh hay or chewing their cuds, was in sharp contrast to the howling wind outside. It was a wonderful feeling: despite difficult circumstances, everything had gone well.

Soon, though, it was time to face the storm again. The plowmen had kept the big diesel running while I was treating my patient, and were all set to venture back. With John's words of gratitude warming my heart, I started up the car and started the long, cold journey home.

# 7

# Two For the Price of One

One beautiful May morning, Duncan Campbell, an elderly farmer in the heart of King's County, phoned me at about seven o'clock in the morning. He wanted his yearling colt "attended to" as soon as possible. This was not an unusual request. Every spring, a large number of farmers wanted their animals "attended to" — a polite way of saying "castrated." My wife, Connie, took most of the calls, and farmers in those days were always polite to the ladies. A newly freshened cow who retained the afterbirth, for instance, was delicately referred to as an animal who "didn't do well." Connie would surprise the farmers by using the correct terminology: "How many days has she retained the afterbirth?" The reply would be: "Oh, well, it's been two or three days, and she hasn't done well yet."

Duncan Campbell was as polite as the next man, and he had a second request that he couldn't discuss, even with me. "By the way," he said, "I have another little job for you to do, but I can't tell ya over the phone."

"Okay, Duncan," I replied. "I hope I'll have the supplies I'll need for that little job. I'll go down as soon as breakfast is finished. Is that soon enough?"

There was silence on the line for a moment. Then he asked, "You mean you ain't et yet?"

"No, we're a little slow today, but I should be down in about half an hour."

Duncan Campbell, farmer, 1957

"All right, if that's the best you can do."

I figured that Duncan probably had been up since about five o'clock. Surely getting the colt "attended to" wasn't that urgent? Apparently the other undertaking he had in mind was, and perhaps had even kept him awake half the night.

I got ready as fast as I could. I was happy to be on the road that morning in my little Volkswagen. The drive to Duncan's farm in Woodville Mills was a delightful one. The Island is always beautiful in spring, and under the early morning sun, it is at its best. The country was springing to life. Pastures were turning green; new leaves were appearing on the trees; farmers were in the fields mending fences; women were hanging laundry on their clotheslines. Road machines on the red clay roads were smoothing deep fissures made during the spring run-off. By the time I arrived at Duncan's farm, I was in a wonderful mood.

Duncan was not. When I drove up his lane, I could see him pacing in front of the horse stable, a fork in his hand. "How are you today, Duncan?" I asked. "Not bad," he replied, not smiling. "Thought you'd never get here."

"Where is this wild bronco that you want changed, Duncan?"

"He's in the horse stable, but he's grown an inch or two since I called ya."

I could tell the man was worried about the operation — or possibly about some other issue. He was very much on edge.

"Go get half a bucket of water," I told him, "and we will get right at the operation."

In the 1950s, there were no good tranquilizers or narcotics for horses, so most veterinarians did this surgery with the help of a tail hitch and a twitch (a chain looped over a horse's nose), which distracted the animal momentarily. A neighbour had come to Duncan's farm to help restrain the colt. With the twitch firmly placed on the nose, and the tail hitch pulling the rear quarters, I performed the operation in about a minute.

"My God, man, you're not done, are ya?" Duncan could not believe that a colt could be castrated while standing. In the old days, there would be about six men with ropes, casting the animal and binding the legs tightly to ensure that nobody got hurt.

"Let the twitch go, Duncan. I'll let the tail go and give him a tetanus shot and an antibiotic to prevent any infection."

"That's wonderful, Doc, but are you sure you had time to get them both out?"

"Look over by the wall. Don't you see both organs?"

"By God, there they are. I'll be damned!"

Once that job was done to his satisfaction, Duncan was in a better mood. I seemed to have restored his confidence in my ability. But he was still a little on edge. Finally, he blurted out the reason.

"Look here, Doc," he said, "I have this damn aching tooth, and since you did such a good job on the horse, I know this tooth would be nothing for you to fix. Besides, my car ain't percolatin' too good, and dentists charge a lot, ya know."

I tried to explain that dental extraction was quite a different procedure from castration. Besides, I wasn't qualified to pull human teeth. And, anyway, my dental equipment was back at the office.

Duncan would not take no for an answer. "Look," he said, "I'll sit with my back agin' the old oak here, and you put your knee on my chest and yank!"

Sensing that I might be persuaded, he added, "Look, I've got me new fencing pinchers right here. I figured you might not have the right tools. These boys will pull any tooth in your head."

"Okay," I said finally, "get over by that tree, and if you think these pliers will do the job, I'll take a crack at it."

Leaning against the tree, Duncan opened his mouth wide. I grasped the pliers and, with a quick jerk, yanked out a big lower molar. The whole procedure took about the same amount of time as the castration. There was a bit of bleeding, so I headed to the car for some cotton to fill the gap in my patient's mouth.

"Don't need no cotton, Doc," he said. "Have some flour in my pocket. Figured it might come in handy."

I happened to have a camera in the car that day, and before I left the farm, I took a photograph of Duncan, grinning now, and proudly holding up the makeshift dental tool and the bad tooth. I figured nobody would believe that I had been practising dentistry on my two-legged clients.

I needn't have worried. It wasn't long before I was famous throughout that part of the county for something besides veterinary medicine. Duncan told just about everybody he knew about his experience. "Ya know," he told one neighbour, "that vet has a powerful set of arms. He should have been a dentist."

# 8

# The Bug

"**I** know the road isn't open, Doctor, but you've got a Volkswagen." This was a remark I often heard on the phone in the mid-1950s, when the mighty Volkswagen Bug first appeared on the Island. The Bug was the car most veterinarians used during the days of little pavement and much snow and mud.

I bought my first Bug in the winter of 1955 — for $1,450 — on the advice of Dr. George Inman, a family physician in Montague. We had moved the clinic to Montague the previous year, and by then I was responsible for veterinary service to the entire county. I desperately needed reliable transportation. Dr. Inman had bought a Volkswagen and loved to demonstrate how well the little car could traverse ditches, cross plowed fields, and make it back on the road in one piece. "It's truly amazing how well they ride over rough fields," he said one day, picking an alder limb from the rear bumper. "The independent suspension on all four wheels is great."

Our Dodge wagon had only about six inches of clearance, leaving the oil pan vulnerable during rough travelling. On cold winter mornings, we had to use hot water to thaw out frozen gearshift levers. The traction was poor, as was the six-cylinder engine. Dr. George's demonstration convinced me that the Bug was the secret weapon to conquer the miles and miles of gutted snow and mud that Islanders called roads.

Bud's Bug with unidentified men in Lorne Valley, 1957

One cold March evening, Wilfred Furness of Vernon Bridge called about a maternity case in the cow stable. "I can't get the calf, and I think the calf bed is twisted," he said. "Lloyd can find the head but no feet." Wilfred's son Lloyd managed the large Ayrshire herd with his father. "The road through Kinross is bad, so you better come around by Millview."

"Okay," I said, knowing that the connecting road to the farm was only a single plowed path. "Looks like a Caesarean section," I told Connie, hanging up the phone. "Better not wait up."

The snow thickened as I headed to the town road. Puddles of snowy ice-water splashed over the windshield, freezing as it hit. De-icing devices were unknown in those early Volkswagens, so I had to stop regularly to scrape the ice off the windshield. I could tell the little car was icing up badly, because the front end wasn't responding to the steering wheel, but I finally made it to the Furness farm.

In the stable, I gradually turned the cow's uterus around, and, using calving chains, pulled a baby heifer calf into the world. "Lucky we didn't have to do a section,"

Lloyd said, helping to lift up the new arrival for Mom to lick clean.

Then it was time for the trip home. Lloyd cleaned off the ice from the front end of the car with a crowbar. "Better stop at Dan's," he said. "See if the road's open, and come back for the night if it's blocked."

Dan Cummings ran the general store in Vernon Bridge. He was just closing up for the night when I pulled in. "The road to Millview is blocked, so the only way you're going to get home tonight, Buddy-boy, is down the railway track. The train plow just went through, and you might possibly get to the town road." I thought of Dr. George and the plowed fields.

"Thanks, Dan," I said, and off I went. I can still see Dan laughing and waving as my little Bug took off down the freshly plowed train track. I could hardly believe my luck: my faithful little car was the same width as the train!

By the time I reached the ninety-degree turn to Montague, the front wheels were so iced up, they were almost impossible to turn. Five or six times, I got out and kicked off more frozen snow and ice, each attempt giving me a bit more steering ability. After making the turn, I still had the hurdle of Bell's Hill, a steep grade at any time of year. Weighted down with ice, would the Bug make it? Barely, at five miles an hour, in first gear. The final mile home was heavy going, with cross winds and heavy snow. "Keep going, little Bug," I prayed. At last, Montague!

In Montague, I put the Bug inside a service station for the night. "Where the devil did you come from, man?" asked my good friend and mechanic Doug Coffin. "Looks like you came from the North Pole."

The next morning, Doug's assistant, Stewart Westaway, estimated he had cleaned 800 pounds of ice from the car. As I silently gave thanks for my safe journey, I thought I could hear Dr. George whisper, "I told you they were amazing."

# 9

# The Brown Trap Door

On a bitter-cold February night in the mid-1950s, the phone rang just before midnight. "Hi, Doc, this is John MacDonald. I got a bad problem. My pigs are all dying!" His voice was a bit slurred. I wasn't sure whether this was due to a few drinks or to a speech impediment. "I hate to drag you out on such a miserable cold, stormy night, Doc, but you gotta help me."

He might have had a bad problem, but I had several. Looking out the window, I could see that the snow was blowing around briskly. Mr. MacDonald's farm, on the north side of the Island, was thirty miles away. The snowplow may have gone through, but the narrow cuttings could fill in quickly. I wasn't sure that I could make a round trip of sixty miles in that weather. However, I seldom turned down a farmer in an emergency.

"Which one of the John MacDonalds are you?" I asked. There were at least twenty-five John MacDonalds in the Souris area, and one always had to check. Some had nicknames by way of identification, and some were known by the names of their fathers and grandfathers, in addition to their own. "This is John Dan Reggie, you know, just past the school on the left."

His voice was even more slurred now. Obviously had a few too many, I thought, but one shouldn't judge a person in trouble.

"Could you give me some details?" I asked "What seems to be the trouble with your pigs?

"I-I-I don't rightly know," he stammered. "T-t-two died this morning, and there's five or six more sick. I just know they will be dead in the morning." He sounded as though he were almost at the point of tears. "Will ya come up? I'll pay ya! I know you have one of those little foreign cars — they'll go through anything."

There was little doubt that Volkswagens were good on bad roads, but there is a limit to what any car can do in drifting snow and poor visibility. I glanced at my watch. This was going to be an all-night trip, I thought. "All right, Mr. MacDonald," I said, "I'll try to make it up to your place. Would you please hang the lantern to a post so I'll have some idea where your gate is?"

By the time I left the house, the thermometer read 15 below zero. I had no idea what the wind chill was, but the radio said the wind was gusting to 40. My trusty Volkswagen started without any trouble, and I muttered a prayer of thanks that my friend Francis Rudisch, the mechanic who serviced my car, had installed a gas-burning heater a month earlier. Still, it was a dirty night. Heavy snowfall, plus the high winds, made visibility almost non-existent. The Seven-Mile Road leading to MacDonald's farm had been plowed earlier in the evening, but at midnight the cuttings were narrowing badly. The snow blew off the windshield most of the time, but when I hit a heavy drift, a fluffy white cloud clung to the glass, and I had to stop often to clean it off.

As I reached the intersection at Dingwell's Mills, the half-way point, I spotted flashing lights on the road leading east to Souris. If I was lucky enough to catch that plow, I thought, maybe the operator would go ahead of me, north to St. Margaret's. When the plow operator pulled into a service station, I caught up with him, jumped out, and climbed up on the cab of the big machine.

"What in the devil are you doing out on a night like this?" the operator asked.

"I have to go up the Bear River road to John McDonald's," I said. "He's got pigs dying!" "Which John McDonald?" "It's John Dan Reggie, near the school." "Oh yeah, we know exactly where it is. Follow us, we'll drive the plow right to the barn."

I thanked the plow driver fervently, and off we went. By then, the snow was flying so thick, it was hard to pick out the riding lights on the big rig. Now, there's an obliging man, I said to myself as I followed the plow. If there were ever two types of people destined for sainthood, it had to be telephone operators and plowmen. In time of emergency or trouble of any sort, these were people you could depend on. Tonight was a typical occasion. Several times, we had to stop because the visibility was so poor. More than once, the plow came close to leaving the clay road, because it was impossible to tell where the centre was. Many times, the driver had to reverse his machine and punch a path through the high drifts. Obviously, I never would have made it on my own. "Thank God I met the plow," I mused. "What would I have done?"

When in difficulty, I often prayed silently for guidance, or turned to the hymns of my youth. On this wild night, I began singing softly: *Brightly beams our Father's mercy, from His lighthouse evermore, trying now to make the harbour, in the darkness may be lost.* That old melody comforted and reassured me.

When I reached the upper end of the Bear River road, I was relieved to see a tall steeple, looming in the sky. That would be St. Margaret's Church, and would mean we had only about a mile and a half to go. As our route turned west, the drifts were at right angles to the road, and the big diesel unit ahead had little difficulty gouging a trail, piling snow eight to ten feet high. Big clumps of snow rolled into my path from the tall cuttings on either side, but the solid pan bottom of my little gem of a car flattened these obstacles with ease.

Suddenly a left turn brought us to MacDonald's farm. There was the old lantern, hanging on a post in the yard. The plow boys hollered, "We'll wait for you, because that road will fill in fast along here." "Thanks," I shouted back, "I'll be as fast as possible."

With some regret, I climbed out of my lovely warm car and into the bone-chilling cold. Grabbing my carry-all from the back seat, I ran over and picked up the lantern and made my way to the house. Everything was in darkness. Either the farmer had fallen asleep or he had given up hope that I would arrive. I hammered on the kitchen door three or four times. No response. In desperation, I kicked the outer door open and yelled, "Is there anybody home?"

From one of the back rooms came a sound of a body falling over a table or chair, accompanied by cuss words. Then I heard the sounds of a person making his way to the kitchen door. I held up the lantern, but its globe was covered with soot after being in the high wind, and gave only a glimmer of light.

"Who the hell are you?" asked the man in the house. He appeared to be quite drunk.

"I'm the doctor you sent for," I said.

"Oh my God — I didn't think you could make it in this awful storm!"

"The government plow opened the road for me," I told him. "Now, let's see those sick pigs."

"I could use a doctor myself," he drawled, burping. "This damn home brew gave me the runs. I don't dare put me pants on, Doc."

This was one of the times when I felt like walking out of a case. This one was bordering on the ridiculous.

Instead, I grabbed my flashlight from the carry-all. "Get your coat on," I said. "It's cold outside." The farmer

managed to get a coat on while scurrying across the barn-
yard. When he reached the pig barn, he tripped over the
crowbar that kept the door shut, cursed under his breath,
and finally made his way to where the pigs were.

I knew at a glance what the problem was. The poor
animals had red, diamond-shaped skin eruptions all over
them, a clear case of erysipelas, an infectious bacterial
disease.

"Did the pigs eat anything today, John?" I asked.

"Don't know, but I'll find out."

Attempting to clear the straw that had accumulated
in the trough, John fell head-first into the half-frozen,
slimy mess. For a few moments, he was stuck solid, too
drunk to move. Worse, his coat had slipped over his head.
What that revealed was a huge brown-stained mass on his
"Stanfield's trap door."

I treated the remaining hogs with serum and penicillin, got the poor, famished pigs some water and stomach
powder, and packed my medical chest for the trip home.
By then, John had sobered up considerably. He started
toward the house. "I gotta pay ya," he said. "I don't expect you to come all this way on such a night for nothing." Disappearing in the dark room, he returned with the
money. "I'm much obliged that ya came up, Doc," he said,
flicking pigfeed from one ear. "I'll remember ya for this!"

I pocketed my $12 fee, trudged through the drifts to
the snowplow, and tapped on the window of the big machine, waking two very tired operators, "Let's roll, boys,"
I said.

"We'll take you to Dingwell's Mills, Doc. We were
talking to the Dundas plow over the two-way radio, and
the boys will take you to Poole's Corner."

I thanked them for their help, climbed into my warm,
still-running car, and waved good-bye to John, and off we
went into the night. By then, the storm was slowly abat-
ing. On my way home, I began to reflect on the events of

the night. That farmer should have called me twenty-four hours earlier. But I realized that, like many others, he had waited to call the doctor until he was desperate — and that often meant a cry for help late at night, when troubles seem to get worse.

In responding to that call, I could have frozen to death, stuck in a snowdrift miles from any form of shelter except for the trusty little Volkswagen "Bug." Then again, if I had refused to make the trip, a small herd of swine probably would have died a painful death. I would not have had the pleasure of meeting John Dan Reggie MacDonald. And I would have missed out on yet another instance of being rescued by the "road angels" — those dedicated snowplow operators who always seemed to be in the right place at the right time.

Ah, yes, I thought, as my little car plowed through the snow, toward home, safety, and breakfast. It was great to be alive. And yes, great to be a country vet.

# 10

## Mud, Sweat and Tears

For a veterinarian spending most of his days on the road, winter driving could be hazardous in the 1950s, but spring driving was a challenge of another kind. Sometimes a client would meet me at the beginning of an impassible road with a horse and cart, a horse and wagon, or a tractor. Once I found a horse tied to a tree with an attached note: "Please take Dolly and bring her home. I'm using the sleigh to clean the barn."

One night in the spring of 1955, a call came from an East Point farmer with a cow that was trying to give birth. By then, I was based in Montague, about forty-five miles away, and I was still the only practitioner in the county. The season was typical of the Island: cold, wet, and muddy. The road to the east end of the Island was impassable. The only possible way to see the animal was to travel west all the way to Charlottetown, and then east to East Point — a distance of ninety-seven miles. By the time I left for East Point, it was 2 a.m. I had to drive home — again by way of Charlottetown — in a dense fog. When I arrived back in Montague at 9 a.m., Connie informed me that another cow had been trying to freshen, and that she had been at it most of the night. Where was the farm located? Of course. Next-door to the one I had left a couple of hours earlier. I could think of only one response: "Better make me some toast. I have to get going."

Veterinarians were always on the road in the spring. Cows were bred to freshen early, to take advantage of the early summer green pastures. Most of the milk that was sold was produced in the early summer. One day Lloyd MacDonald, a dairy farmer in Kinross, about eight miles west of Montague, phoned to say that his cows were calving, and he needed help.

"There's a bit of soft mud on the road plus a few little ponds," Lloyd told me on the phone, "but nothing to stop a Volkswagen."

That winter, there had been a lot of snow, and most of the north-south roads were nearly impossible to keep open. And when the high banks of snow thawed, the clay roads turned to porridge.

The road to Lloyd MacDonald's farm was so thick with red mud, the drive seemed to take forever. I discovered that truckloads of potatoes and livestock had managed to churn up gumbo about two feet deep. The worst section, a quarter-mile stretch between Lloyd's and the Orwell Head cemetery, turned out to be a real test of his faith in the ability of the Volkswagen to get through anything.

I did manage to make it to the maternity ward at Lloyd's, and after an uneventful delivery, I packed my gear into the car and headed for home.

I didn't get far. I soon dropped into a mud puddle that swallowed up my little car. Lloyd arrived, shovel in hand, shaking his head. "You get in and gun her, and I'll grab a-hold of your bumper," he said.

I had the feeling one person would never budge my mini-sub, so I got out of the car and surveyed the scene. There were no tractors available, as farmers had taken the batteries out for the winter. Finally, we decided that if I left the engine running, put the car in low gear, and helped push, we might just move it.

"That looks simple enough," Lloyd said. "But what if she takes off on us? That darn car will be in Uigg before you can catch up with it. And with those big rubber boots on, you'll be pretty slow." He did have a point. The car might take off for Uigg, the next community, without me. Still, I replied, with a confidence I didn't feel: "Leave it to me, Lloyd. I have a plan — if I can move fast enough."

Starting the little car, I put her in first gear, jumped out and grabbed the bumper.

"My God, she's going, Doc! Get in quick!" Unfortunately, I couldn't hop in fast enough; the car was going five miles an hour by then. My only hope was to resort to Plan B — jumping on the bumper and lifting the engine bonnet, which, of course, was in the back of the car — and removing the coil wire in the centre of the distributor cap. Mission accomplished. The car was stopped in her tracks, and luckily had gone far enough to land on high ground. I managed to get home safely, although I never did get the mud out of that car.

In a way, there wasn't much use in trying to clean the car. I had many more muddy miles ahead of me — and, in fact, behind me. Normally the mud season on the Island was long enough, but that year, it had started early. Toward the end of January, after months of heavy snowfall, we had a big thaw. To use a typical Island expression, the bottom "went completely out" of the clay roads.

During the thaw, my friend Doug Aitken, a dairy-and-potato farmer from Fortune, passed away. I decided to go to his funeral at the little church in Bay Fortune, but the road to the church had been newly rebuilt and was reported to be impassible. "You'll never make it through Little Pond," warned Rand MacDonald, the storekeeper near Annandale. "I heard the road machine got stuck there this morning." Not heeding Rand's warning, I foolishly said, "What the hell, I'll try it anyway."

On the newly graded road, mud was splashing continually on the windshield. Because the Bug had no window-washing system, I had to stop periodically to throw snow on the glass. Then I reached the spot where the snowplow got stuck. I hit bottom. My wheels spun wildly, but I was going nowhere.

Luckily, three brawny farmers were loading hay on a wagon in a nearby field, and came over to help. Sheepishly, I asked for a push.

"When we lift, Mister, you give her hell and don't stop," one of them instructed, apparently ready to throw that little tin can into orbit.

"I'm ready," I said, ramming the Bug into first gear. With an ungodly roar and mud flying everywhere, we had liftoff. Looking back, I caught a glimpse of three men laughing their heads off, completely covered in red gravy and pointing to the black Bug, skimming along as though nothing had happened.

I had two more miles to go, dodging the deep fissures in the road every few feet. As I rounded the last turn to Bay Fortune, I saw the church. There were no cars parked outside — just a few horses and wagons and tractors and trailers. One tractor pulled the hearse to the cemetery, and another hauled a two-ton truck loaded with family, pallbearers, and friends. Apparently this end of the road was also considered impassible.

After the service I decided to get off the clay road as soon as possible and head for the pavement. Once again, I made it home the long way around — driving all the way west to Charlottetown and then back east to Montague. I figured my little wonder car had performed enough heroic deeds for the day.

# 11

## "I steered him with a ring"

"There's a man on the phone who keeps yelling at the top of his lungs," Connie told me, "and I haven't the slightest idea what he's talking about — something about a ring and steering."

Connie, secretary and general manager of our clinic, was quite capable of taking messages from farmers, but the gentleman on the phone didn't seem to be making much sense. I took the phone. It was a man with a pronounced English accent, which probably explained some of Connie's difficulty in understanding him.

"This is John Denhem from the Whim Road," the caller said. "I've steered my bull with a ring, and he's in bad shape."

Johnny Denhem was known in this area as "the English farmer." He had served in the Royal Air Force and had met an Island woman while stationed at the navigation school in Charlottetown during the Second World War. After the war, the Denhems settled down on a farm near Montague, and he worked as a farmer and bricklayer. From time to time, the farming side gave him a few problems.

"What do you mean, you 'steered him with a ring'?" I asked.

"Well, I'll tell you, you see, I bought this bull from a farmer down the road about a month ago, and he told me that I should have him steered. I guess on the Island they call it castration. All I know is that a cattle trader came here about a month ago and steered him for me using a rubber band. My God, you should see him, Doctor. His organs are bigger than ever. One is even touching the ground."

I found the story almost unbelievable. The use of rubber bands for castration was a controversial and cruel practice. In very young animals they were used routinely in the 1950s, with mixed results. I was totally opposed to the idea. Performing such a procedure by simply cutting off the circulation and letting the whole area "rot off" was not only downright cruel, it was also risky. I felt that these practices should have been outlawed years before.

"I'll be out to see the animal right away," I assured the caller. "But I wish you had called me a month ago. It sounds like one terrible mess."

When I arrived at the farm a few minutes later, my worst fears were confirmed. The poor animal, about a year old, had an appendage hanging between his hind legs to about two inches above the ground. Nature attempts to heal a traumatized area by sending more blood to the site, and this causes swelling. In this instance, the animal's scrotal organs were about ten times their normal size. He had failed terribly from the ordeal. It was one of the worst messes I had ever seen. It made as much sense to me as if a doctor had tried to remove someone's finger by tying a cord around it and letting the part rot off.

"My goodness, John," I said, "whoever did this should be charged with cruelty to animals. I'll try to remove the total mass, but the animal will have to undergo an anaesthetic."

It took the best part of an hour to remove the large, traumatized organ. The rubber band ended up costing the farmer about ten times the amount of a proper castration. Besides the surgery, the animals needed aftercare and antibiotics to clear up the infection. For a long time, it was questionable whether the poor steer would be able to urinate. Although he eventually came around and began to put on weight, the loss of six months' growth was another cost to the farmer.

The incident also cost John years of remorse, knowing that he had inadvertently allowed an injustice perpetrated against a helpless creature that had been entrusted to his care. After a couple of years had passed, I happened to meet him in a local grocery store. Almost tearfully, he confessed that he was ashamed of having to call me to bring some relief to the steer. "And I grew up in England, where that kind of cruelty is outlawed!" he said.

"Never mind, John," I said. "Don't blame yourself. Quite often innocent people are victims of bad advice, but you managed to do the right thing in calling for help."

Unfortunately, the barbaric practice of rubber-band surgery continued for decades on some Island farms, especially for docking lambs' tails, much to the dismay of the veterinary profession, and in spite of documented cases of serious infection.

But "the English farmer" had learned a hard lesson. Never again did he allow "steering with a ring."

# 12

## Red Ointment Magic

Sometimes in medicine, strange and wonderful things happen. Take the case of the Campbell cows, for instance.

The Campbells, an elderly brother and sister, carried on a modest farm operation near the wharf at Newport, a small coastal village in the central part of King's County, where a ferry used to carry produce and people to the railway line across the bay in Georgetown. The Campbells had a milking herd of six or seven cows, some young "fat cattle," and a number of swine.

One spring day in 1957, I received an urgent call from Mr. Campbell. "This Bessie cow freshened a few days ago," he told me on the phone, "and for the life of me I can't get the weed out of her bag. I've bathed and rubbed some lard on it to soften it, but it's no better."

The term "weed" was used in the old days to describe hardness and chronic swelling of the udder. When I arrived at the farm, I discovered that Bessie had a very bad case of mastitis, or inflammation of the udder. The infection was compounded by the fact that the attachment of her large, pendulous udder had broken down. "We have to get the infection under control with drugs, Mr. Campbell," I said, "and this udder needs more hot applications and a softening ointment, applied twice daily."

"My God, man," he replied, "I'll have to get Mary to help me. You know, my arms are damn near played out from rubbing Bessie."

The poor folks had a difficult task ahead of them. The disease was well advanced, and saving Bessie would require a lot of care. "You must bathe the udder at least two or three times a day, Mary," I told her, "and rub this red ointment into the udder for at least twenty minutes after bathing." The ointment, generally used for cuts and scrapes to stimulate epithelial growth, had as its main ingredient a substance called "scarlet red."

Mary gave me a suspicious look. "I don't have a lot of faith in ointments," she said. "Look at my hands, covered with eczema for years. I must have put on twenty or more kinds of ointments, and I'm no better. But I'll give this a try, Doctor, if you say so."

I showed Mary the proper massage method. Hand pressure must start at the bottom of the pendulous udder and press upward, taking the fluid away from the base and gently forcing the liquid into the animal's system.

As I was leaving the farm, I told Mr. Campbell that I would be back in a couple of days to check on the cow.

"We'll work on her, Doc," he said, "and as long as my sister's arms hold out, we'll give old Bessie the best of care."

I knew that the Campbells meant what they said. Being of Scottish lineage, they were a determined lot. Their ancestors had settled on this land a few generations before, and had been able to survive many a challenge.

A couple of days later, I pulled into the farmyard. Mary came running over to the car, waving her hands over her head. "Oh my goodness," I thought. "The poor animal must have died, and Mary doesn't want me to go to the stable."

What puzzled me, though, was Mary's ecstatic tone of voice. "Doctor, Doctor, look at my hands! Look! Look!"

Not having ever paid much attention to Mary's hands, I asked about the cow. "How's Bessie doing?"

"Look! My eczema's gone!" Mary exclaimed. "It's a miracle, Doctor! The cow's great, and my hands are all healed up! It's all thanks to that red wonder ointment. I've told the whole neighbourhood, including Father MacDonald. Nobody ever thought I would be cured. Oh, if it hadn't been for Bessie getting sick, I would be just the same. Oh, Doctor, it's a miracle!"

I had never imagined that I could create a miracle, even with my red magic ointment. What had saved Bessie, I was sure, was the faithful therapy carried out by the Campbells. By accident, the ointment had contained just the right ingredients to cure Mary's eczema. As most people with a skin condition know, a person can try a long list of treatments before finding one that helps.

In any case, Mary and her neighbours seemed to have great faith in this particular treatment. Before long, sales of the red ointment soared. I heard that it was being used for every sore and abrasion in the Newport area.

Years later, after the Campbell farm was shut down and some of the family had died, Mary was still keeping in touch. One day, while on an extended trip to the West Coast, I received a letter from her, with a twenty-dollar bill inside. The note said: "Please send a couple of jars of that magic red ointment, as I have two of my friends on the salve, and they are almost cured of the dreaded eczema."

By that time, I had attended hundreds of sick animals, and had prescribed countless doses of medicine for various ailments. But nothing before or after my visit to the Campbell farmer created excitement equal to the stir caused by my "magic red ointment."

# 13

## Poor Mike

The call came on a beautiful, sunny October morning, one of those glorious early fall days when the light seems touched with gold. Unfortunately, the voice of the farmer on the phone, John Cuddy, did not match the mood of the day. In fact, he sounded close to tears. "My best horse, the Clyde, is not right," he said. "For the last few days Mike hasn't been eating like he should. He always eats like a horse should, but this morning he didn't even eat his oats."

I assured Mr. Cuddy that I would leave right away for his farm, which was about ten miles south of our clinic. As I drove there, down one of the Island's few paved roads, I gathered my thoughts about Mr. Cuddy's dilemma. His Clydesdale horse was only five years old. Why would he be reluctant to eat? Perhaps it was a case of simple indigestion. His owner was what we called "a real horse person," knowledgeable about his animals and careful to look after them properly.

Driving past the bird sanctuary, I smiled at the sight of flocks of black ducks and geese on the pond, sheltered by dark spruce and flaming maple trees, and resting peacefully in the sun. No worries in their world, I thought.

It was a different story when I turned onto a clay road and down the lane of the Cuddy farm. The farmer was waiting for me beside the horse barn, his face looking troubled. "Better check his teeth, Doc," he said. "Never had 'em filed. Too young for that." Many young horses have severe dental problems, but I didn't bother to argue that point. "Guess I'd better have a look, Mr. Cuddy. I'll get the speculum to hold his mouth open."

There seemed to be nothing wrong with the horse's mouth. He walked without difficulty. And other physical signs were normal. However, his temperature was about half a degree above normal. Something was not right.

One of my professors in veterinary school once said, "Treat the obvious, and worry about the rest." I pumped some colic cure — mineral oil and turpentine — into Mike's stomach through his nose and gave him a shot of antibiotics. Then I left the farm, instructing Mr. Cuddy to call me in the morning if Mike showed no improvement. It was still a mystery to me. There must be some cause for that elevated temperature. Still, what's half a degree?

The next morning, Mr. Cuddy phoned again. This time, his voice was shaking, and pitched a notch higher than normal. "Mike can't move now, Doc," he said. "Ya gotta come on down right away."

As I drove to the Cuddy farm, the sky above me was dark, and rain splattered on my windshield. The change in the weather seemed like an ominous sign. At this point, I was worried: I had a feeling that we were dealing with a case of tetanus. What else would bring on such sudden symptoms?

My worst fears were confirmed when I walked into the barn. Poor Mike had developed a full-blown case of tetanus, or lockjaw, as it was commonly called. I had neglected to ask whether he had ever stepped on a sharp object, and Mr. Cuddy hadn't mentioned it. Most people don't think to mention something that happened two or three months previously — about the time for the incubation of the soil-borne bacteria to produce the symptoms we were seeing. Mr. Cuddy scratched his head, and then blurted, "Gosh, Doc, I forgot. He did step on a board with a nail in it about three months ago. I forgot all about it."

Everything was falling into place now: the muscle stiffness yesterday and now the nervousness, higher temperature, indigestion. If further evidence were required, I saw that the horse's jaws were clamped shut, and the third eyelid was prolapsed.

Reluctantly, I gave Mr. Cuddy the bad news. The mortality rate for tetanus was 75 to 80 per cent, even with many doses of anti-toxins and antibiotics. And the time to give the anti-toxins was at the time of the puncture wound, which also should have been drained properly. Now it was too late. We really should put Mike down, I told his owner.

"I can't do it, Doc," Mr. Cuddy said quietly. "Not today. I just can't see poor Mike put to sleep."

I felt sorry for the farmer, but pleaded with him not to prolong Mike's agony. He was able to drink a little water, but was totally unable to move his jaws. I knew he would be even worse the next day.

The next morning, Mr. Cuddy called again. He told me sadly that he wanted me to come to the farm one more time.

This time, I felt sad and frustrated on that now-familiar drive. My task would be to end the life of a poor young gelding, a faithful servant who could have been saved by a little medication and care at the proper time.

# 14

## Full Circle

The calving season always coincided with the spring season. Farmers planned it this way. The idea was to have cows in a peak period of production when the pastures were lush and green. Milk and cheese factories operated only during the summer, when milk production was at its best. For veterinarians, calving season meant constant travel, on roads that took a heavy toll on mind, spirit, and vehicle.

One beautiful Sunday afternoon in mid-April, I had a call from George Tweedy, a farmer from Earnscliffe, about twenty miles west of our clinic. "I have a cow with the calf bed prolapsed," he said. "Could you come up right away?" I told him I would. "How's the road?" I asked. The main road between Montague and Charlottetown was paved, but George lived on a long, muddy side road. George promised to meet me with his tractor and trailer at the Cherry Valley corner, a few minutes' drive from his road. I had a feeling this might be a long afternoon.

George was waiting for me at the corner, his vehicles covered in red mud. "My Lord, George, where did you get all that mud?" I asked. "You'll see lots of that before you get back here," he drawled, a smile spreading across his ruddy, weather-beaten face. "There are a couple of other lads looking for you, too. The Mutches have a cow down with milk fever, and McInnises have a sick calf, so you'd better bring lots of stuff."

I grabbed my surgical kit, carry-all, and drug suitcase, and climbed aboard. Turning down George's road toward the Northumberland Strait, the little Massey-Ferguson tractor slopped past the country store, where a big white cat was sunning herself in the window. "You lucky thing," I thought, smiling.

When we drove into George's farmyard, he ran to the house for warm water and towels, and I carried my equipment to the stable. In a box stall, I examined a cow that was lying down, her womb completely prolapsed. "I guess I should have shot her," George said, his eyes filling with tears. "She's my best cow, so I thought she should have a chance to live." I gave the cow an epidural of procaine, a nerve block that stops straining, makes the animal more comfortable, and makes it possible to replace the uterus. "Get a halter on her, George," I said. "Let's see if we can get her to her feet. She's a long way from dying."

When we got the cow on her feet, we cleaned and disinfected the womb, and returned it to its proper place. Wearing shoulder-length rubber gloves, I inserted disinfectant tablets and stainless-steel pins to prevent further prolapsing. Then I gave the cow a bottle of calcium solution to prevent milk fever, which also can lead to a prolapsed womb. By then, the cow looked well, and so did George. "I'm much obliged, Doc," he said. "I had little hope in the beginning. You sure did me a favour!"

I had just cleaned up and packed my gear when Frank Mutch walked in the door. Frank was a big, lanky farmer who lived about half a mile down the same road. "Good to see you, Doc," he said. "I have a cow trying to push her head through the stall. What's it sound like?" George teased him: "Must be spring fever. This is the time of year for it, Frank." I told Frank a number of conditions could cause those symptoms. "Guess we better go and have a look."

This time, our conveyance was a horse and wagon. As we headed for Frank's farm, the mud kept getting deeper. "Damn road isn't fit to put a horse on," Frank growled under his breath. "I never saw the road so bad. It'll be June before it dries up."

At the barn, Frank led me to a Holstein cow. She was in her third lactation — that is, calving for the third time — and obviously very nervous. A physical examination turned up nothing to indicate her trouble. But a urine sample showed that she had nervous acetonemia — in laymen's terms, her system had gone sour. Heavy producers can become acedocic, unable to manufacture enough sugar-related substances. Some animals develop signs of nervousness as part of the brain becomes involved. "Let's put a halter on her," I said, "and I'll inject some dextrose into the jugular vein." On these adventures I usually travelled with as few drugs as possible, but luckily I had happened to bring a bottle of dextrose.

The change in the cow was dramatic. The signs of nervousness disappeared, and she began to eat her hay. "It's like a miracle," Frank said. He removed the halter and let the cow go. She looked perfectly normal. I reminded him to pick up some propylene glycol and to give the cow a cup twice a day.

As I was about to leave the stable, Mrs. Mutch appeared, accompanied by another neighbour, Gerald McInnis. Gerald was a happy fellow, always smiling. "Heard you were in the area," he said. "Those telephone operators have your whereabouts pinned down." Gerald had a cow with milk fever. "I'll see if I have some calcium, Gerald," I said. "We may have to go back to the car." Luck was with me again. An associate had once advised me to always take two bottles of calcium on a call, and he was right.

My third mode of transportation was a horse and sleigh. Climbing aboard, I glanced at my watch. It was

Bud's Bug, Montague, 1957

four o'clock, and the sun was dipping low in the sky over the next district, the coastal community of China Point. This time, we followed a trail through the woods, where the snow was still deep enough for travelling. At least this way, there was no mud. "We don't need mud flaps on this rig," Gerald said with a chuckle. The McInnis farm was on a point of land with high red cliffs overlooking the bay. The wind blowing across the point made the place feel bleak this time of year, although we had a beautiful view across the bay, to the red cliffs of Point Prim, with its lighthouse and snow-capped trees.

The rustic old barns on the McInnis farm were a little twisted, having withstood many gales over the years. "We hope to build a new barn someday," Gerald said. "But you know how hard it is to find money on a farm." Having grown up on a dairy farm, I knew exactly what he meant. Money always seemed to be in short supply.

Gerald's cow had calved earlier that day without problems, but now was unable to stand. "I thought she was coming down with milk fever," Gerald said, tugging at her head. "I felt at dinnertime I had better phone you." It didn't take long to treat this big lady. In about twenty minutes, she jumped to her feet. "That worked wonders, Doc," Gerald said, laughing. "Are you sure you didn't put some holy water in that stuff you gave her?" I replied, "Better than that. This came right off the kitchen stove." For many years, we made up most of the preparations used to treat animals. Connie was an expert at this, and always kept a supply of calcium and other remedies at hand.

As we left the stable, the sun setting in the late-afternoon sky told me that it would soon be dark. Ahead of me was a long, slow journey to the main road. I wondered what mode of transportation we would use this time. Gerald scratched his head. "Guess we'll have to take the horse and cart," he said. "The tractor has a flat tire, and my son is away with the driving wagon."

The trip back was slow. The road-bed was knee-deep, and just the width of the old-fashioned vehicle, a heavy cart with iron wheels, normally used to haul produce around the farm. Gerald's faithful old mare plodded along at a steady pace, never lifting her head or slowing down. The air was getting colder, and, as the mare plunged into this sea of mud, I hoped that the ground wouldn't freeze too quickly.

About half-way to the main road, I noticed a man on horseback, a muffler over his head, waiting by the side of the road. As we were about to pass by, he raised his arm to hail us. "Would you be the vet?" he asked. When he spoke, Gerald recognized him. He was a neighbour, George MacPhee, a quiet, private bachelor who lived with his brother, John. "Got a lovely Hereford calf that can't make it to its feet. Any idea what the matter might be, Doc"? I said I would have to see the animal to be sure. Turning around, George pointed to a small barn and dwelling about half a mile away. "The lane is always blocked — too close to the trees," he said. As the snow was too deep for the cart, it was decided that I should ride George's mare.

When I reached the small barn, I jumped off Dolly and went looking for the sick calf. The little animal was lying on its side, sweating, exhausted, and panting. "Well, I'll be damned," I said to myself. This was the first case of "white muscle disease" I had seen since starting my practice. This condition is caused by a deficiency in selenium, a mineral that acts as a catalyst for the utilization of vitamin E in the muscles. As a result, muscles turn pale and lack strength. If heart muscles are affected, sudden death can occur. I gave the calf some shots of a selenium and vitamin preparation, left the stable, and rode back to my awaiting taxi. I instructed George to treat all the calves born during the season, and he climbed on Dolly's back and headed home.

Driving back to Montague in the dark — in my own car, finally — I thought about the events of this busy Sunday afternoon. Every case was different, as was every form of transportation. It was a memorable day, made even more so because of the people I had met: hardy, resilient folks who took everything in stride, including low incomes, sick animals, stormy weather, and a long, long season dominated by red mud.

# 15

## Queen Lassie's Mistake

I first met Lassie, a black-and-white Border collie, when her owner brought her to the clinic to be spayed. "Now, you be careful with my dog, young fellow," Will Glover said with a smile as he was leaving the clinic, "I don't want anything to happen to her." Will's tone was light, but I knew how important that young dog was to him. Just the fact that he was going to the trouble and expense to have her spayed spoke volumes about his attitude. In those days, it was mostly valuable farm animals — horses, cattle, sheep and pigs — that got to see a veterinarian. Dogs and cats were treated at home, if at all.

In Lassie's case, the surgery went well, and I didn't see her for another couple of years. Then one day Will burst into the clinic, carrying Lassie in his arms. He was close to tears.

It was a sunny, hot day in July, not a rain cloud in sight, a perfect day for making hay, which farmers all over the Island were doing. Will and his boys were no exception. The family had a farm in White Sands, a beautiful property that ran down to the Northumberland Strait. His white house and well-kept barns were a sight to see for anyone passing on the gravel road. Will and his sons milked a dozen cows, and also raised young beef cattle and pigs. The self-appointed supervisor of the livestock was young Lassie.

Bud in Guelph, 1950

As Will explained to me later, Lassie followed Will that day when they drove to the clover field. For a while she had a wonderful time, barking at the seagulls circling overhead, and running circles around the little Ford tractor and mower.

Suddenly there was a sharp yelp. Will quickly stopped the tractor and jumped down. Lassie was lying in front of the mower, licking her foot. It was spurting blood. She had been chasing a bird, and, for a few, fateful seconds, had failed to pay attention to the mower blade. Will's son John, who had heard Lassie howling, was kneeling beside her. It was not a pretty sight. Lassie's foot was almost severed at the ankle.

Will Glover tied a cord tight above the hock to try to control the bleeding, wrapped Lassie's leg in a towel, and raced to the clinic. "I don't know if you can save her foot or not," he said, "but will you please try?"

About a third of the foot was still attached. The remaining tendons were severed and badly torn by the mower blade. "Leave her with me, Will," I said, "and I'll knock her out and give it my best shot."

After a couple of hours of surgery, I sutured the poor little dog's leg back together as best I could. She had lost a great deal of blood, but intravenous fluids soon restored her system. Bandaging and splinting the leg completed my part of the action. "Now, Lassie," I told her, "the rest is up to you."

Two days later, Will came to see his pride and joy. A small dose of tranquilizer kept Lassie from getting too excited when he arrived. Will, on the other hand, was bursting with joy, knowing that his dog was on the mend, and that I hadn't amputated her foot. "There was enough blood flowing to keep Lassie's foot alive," I told him. "I think we'll know for sure in about a week."

A few days after Lassie was discharged from hospital, I happened to be in the area of the Glover farm and called to see the special patient. Lassie had her own hospital room, set up in the dining room. Like a queen on a throne, there she was on her bed, greeting admirers who came to see her from miles around. "The phone has been ringing off the wall ever since the accident," Mrs. Glover said. "People have been coming here all day to see this lady." The rural telephone was doing its work of spreading the news in southern King's County, and Lassie seemed to be enjoying every minute of it.

After that, we had to change the bandages and splints several times, but the foot healed wonderfully. Soon, the pride and joy of the Glover farm was racing around her kingdom and visiting all her subjects.

For years after that, I thought often about that well-loved little Border collie — especially every time I smelled the sweet scent of new-mown clover.

# 16

## If Old Grain Bins Could Talk

In the old days, almost every barn on the Island had a grain bin. Before the days of combines, farmers harvested grain with a binder, and stored the sheaves in a barrack at harvest time. Later, they separated the grain from the straw with a threshing machine, usually threshing a supply of grain and straw bedding which would last a month or two. They stored the grain in a bin, which often was a box that had been used to ship a piano to the home. These boxes would last a lifetime. And they often served a dual purpose.

I was in a cow stable late one night, delivering a calf, when I was introduced to one of those purposes. The call had come in late at night, as often happened during the winter and spring: a cow was having trouble giving birth. Most of the time, we could deliver a calf using a "calving jack," a piece of equipment with a winding mechanism that allowed one person to extract a calf — if all went well in the delivery room. If the calf was in the wrong position, or the mother was too small, that meant a caesarian section. On this particular night, the calving jack didn't work, and as a last resort we had to cut into the cow's flank and deliver the calf through a large incision, a procedure that took about an hour and a half. When it was all over, the farmer said, "I think it's time we paid a little visit to the grain box."

That "little visit" wasn't for the benefit of the cow. In a few minutes, the farmer returned to the stable with a quart of rum. "I think it's time to clear our throats and warm the blood on a cold night like this, whaddya say, Doc?" Thinking about the drive home and the road patrol, I replied, "Sounds like an excellent idea. But just a small one."

"My wife don't allow liquor in the house," the farmer explained. "She hates the stuff. The grain bin is a dandy place to store the booze. It's well-hidden, and I'm the only one that knows it's there."

Scenes of this kind were repeated in barns throughout the county. As I discovered on my rounds, it was no accident that so many farmers decided to head for the barn on a cold winter's night to "check on the horses."

If the bottle wasn't in the grain bin, it would often be kept on top of one of the massive beams in the old barns. I witnessed quite a few pints appearing from the barn loft. After wiping the cobwebs off on his overalls, the farmer might say, "It's a cold night, and I find a mouthful of this great to fight off the flu."

In fact, I did see a case in which the bottle from the grain bin appeared to serve a medicinal purpose. Late one fall night, I got a call from a farmer with a very sick horse. The owner had been plowing a garden that day with the horse, an animal that was only eleven or twelve years old, but was obese and had been idle most of the fall. "I barely got Sam into the barn when he fell down," the farmer told me on the phone. "He's sweating like crazy. Breathing fast, and he looks like he might have had a heart attack. Could you come up? I know it's late, but I'd love to save the old fellow if it's at all possible."

Half an hour later, I arrived at the stable and examined the horse. A urine sample indicated that he had blackwater, an acute and sometimes fatal illness. It is a condition common in horses put to work after a long period of idleness.

Doug Coffin, mechanic (left), and Bob Webster, vet student, 1957

patient decided that he had had enough. With a mighty roar, he headed for the wide-open spaces, taking the old barn sill with him. The old farmer, still clinging to the hundred-foot rope, followed behind as the bull galloped for the shore. He was fast disappearing from view, but we could hear him roaring, "Whoa! Whoa!"

Bob was laughing so hard he could hardly stand up. "Well, Robert," I said, "let's pack up. Looks like we're going to wait to get paid for this call."

Years later, when I met Bob — by then, Dr. Bob — in Charlottetown one day, we began reminiscing about our adventure with the bull. Incidentally, he asked, "did you ever get paid for that operation?"

"No," I replied, "and as far as I know, the old gentleman is still looking for his steer."

# 19

## X-ray Romance

When Laddie, a black Labrador retriever, got hit by a car one afternoon and suffered a fracture of his right hind leg, his owners brought him to my office, which was in the basement of our new house. We had just moved to the Queen's Road in Montague, and our small office was designed mainly to carry clinical supplies for the thousands of livestock located throughout the county. We were equipped to do some small-animal surgery, but this was a very minute part — perhaps five per cent — of veterinary practice in the 1950s. We were not equipped to handle a badly broken leg.

We did, however, have some extra help in the office. George, a senior veterinary student, was doing an internship with us, and had become part of our family for the summer. George and I examined the poor dog to determine the fractured area. "We've got to get an X-ray done," George said. "This looks like a bad smash." I replied that I had no way of getting Laddie X-rayed. "What about the local hospital?" George asked. "Surely they wouldn't mind doing an extra plate?" I said nothing for a few minutes, but thought to myself, "Good heavens above, the medical staff will kill me if I take a dog in for an X-ray!" On the other hand, this dog needed all the help we could give him. "Let's go down and see the lady technician at the hospital," I said. "I know her quite well."

George and I jumped into the station wagon and headed for the hospital to see Ethel, the X-ray technician. When we walked into her office, she asked, "Are you gentlemen here for an examination? I don't believe you have an appointment." George and I smiled. "No, my dear, we don't," I said, "but we're looking for one for Laddie, a Labrador retriever who has a broken leg." Ethel's jaw dropped. "You guys are trying to get me fired," she said, laughing. "I'll have to think about this." At the same time, she was studying George, and I had a feeling she might help. He was a good-looking boy, and she was single. Finally, she said, "Come back tonight about seven, to the back door, and make sure the critter is asleep. I don't want to get eaten." "Don't worry," I told her. "I'll have him out like a light."

That evening, George and I sedated Laddie, carried him to the station wagon on a homemade stretcher, and arrived at the basement door of the hospital at seven sharp. I walked down to the X-ray room to see whether the coast was clear. Ethel was waiting for us. "Bring the boy in," she said. "I'll have to guess at the settings because this is my first critter patient." I was no help, as I had never used an X-ray machine. "Just use your best judgment," I told her. Medical gadgets like this were too expensive for a large-animal practice and seldom needed in the early days of treating pets. Many clients felt that, rather than paying for expensive diagnostic procedures, it might be better to put their animal down. Pets were cheap in those days.

Ethel did a superb job with her canine patient, and we discovered that he had a clean fracture. George and I decided that a plaster-of-Paris cast would repair the break. We thanked Ethel and left for the clinic, borrowing enough material to make a cast. "Be sure to make me a bill for all this, Ethel," I said. "We'll be in touch tomorrow. Thanks for now."

Back at the clinic, the big Lab was starting to wake up,

so George gave him a small dose of the anesthetic that we had inserted through the vein. Then we wrapped the leg with cotton batting and bandages, and applied the plaster of Paris, a procedure that took about an hour.

The next day, two of the hospital medical staff were looking at some X-ray plates. One of them, Dr. Lorne Bonnell, spotted a strange image at one side of the viewer. "What in the world is wrong with that poor creature?" he asked. His colleague, Dr. George Inman, looked closely at the plate. "It must be one of your patients," he said. "It doesn't look belong to anybody I know." After some time, the doctors decided the image must be of some species other than human, but what? "I'll have to ask one of the technicians," Dr. Bonnell said.

To our surprise, Ethel called the clinic that day. "I was just wondering how you were making out with the cast," she said. "I would like to see how it looks on a dog, as I'm used to the human critters." Laughing, I said, "Come on up. We could use some of your expertise." Minutes later, Ethel arrived at the back door, and I took her down to our humble operating room. "My," she said, "this is a neat spot, and that cast looks great." I saw her give George a smile, and I had the feeling George and Ethel were becoming friends.

"Better put something on the cast to stop him from chewing it off," she said. I was pleasantly surprised that she knew that animals did indeed chew their casts off. "I'll put a head collar on him, Ethel, and that will stop him."

Ethel whispered to me, "I think Dr. Bonnell would like to see the cast."

When George, Ethel, and I went upstairs for a cold drink, I knew we had the makings of a beautiful relationship. In fact, it lasted all summer. George and I were able to X-ray quite a few small animals — thanks to a summer romance.

# 20

## The Internet of the Fifties

"If you see a black Volkswagen heading past South Lake, would you run out and tell Bud about the other call in Elmira?" My wife, Connie, who ran our clinic and answered most of the calls from clients, was relaying yet another message through Peggy, the South Lake telephone operator.

It was early spring, and I was travelling in my mud-covered Bug. When I reached South Lake, I spotted Peggy on the road, flapping her phone book to flag me down. "You're the vet, aren't you?" she asked. "That car doesn't look black to me." Then she rubbed a spot on the car with her finger. "Okay, it *is* black, under all that mud. You have to get to Elmira Station. Connie says the cow is worse, and there will be a fellow there to meet you to take you up the lane."

In the days before two-way radios, many rural homes on the Island didn't even have telephones, and I was often on the road. That meant we had to rely on the help of the "telephone angels" — a network of telephone operators in villages throughout the province.

In those days, most of the operators were women, as it seemed that the clear, feminine voice was the one best-suited to the phone system. If you wanted to place a call outside your immediate community, you had to crank the phone to ring "Central," and a helpful operator would connect you to the appropriate household or business. People on the same line could all hear the phone ringing (and could listen to calls if they chose), but each home or business had a specified number of long and short rings that would signal who should answer.

The operators knew just about everything — everybody's phone number, address, habits (good and bad), and often the whereabouts of most people in the neighbourhood. They ordered your telephone, sent notices to you for payment, and collected the account. They could track down the local doctor at the hockey rink or a poker game, round up volunteers to fight a house fire, or direct a veterinarian to an animal in distress.

Connie, staffing the phone from our clinic, knew the county like the back of her hand, and she had to judge calls in order of importance so that I could service as many farmers as possible while I was on the road. The telephone operators were a huge help. Sometimes when a farmer was placing a call to the clinic, they could tell him that I was at so-and-so's farm. The telephone operators were not only an integral part of our practice, but also became part of our family, keeping track of my every move, acting as an answering service, and even, on occasion, offering to babysit.

One nasty April day in 1957, when the clay roads were breaking up badly and a foot of wet snow had just fallen, I was driving to the northeastern part of the county. I was about to make a left turn to Elmira when a woman ran out to the road. It was Helen, the local phone operator. "Wait, Doctor!" she yelled. "I have an urgent message from George Cheverie down the road a couple of miles. His cow is down and could very well be dying. In my opinion, she's far worse than the one at Campbell's in Elmira." Thanking this thoughtful woman, I hurried down the road to George's farm. I felt sure that the "tel-angel" knew what she was talking about.

"How did you get here so quickly?" George asked when I drove in his yard.

"Did you not know," I replied, "that the people of South Lake have a guardian angel looking out for them?"

George was not surprised to learn the identity of the angel. "That's not the first time Helen helped in an emergency," he said. "That same lady has helped save many homes by sending men to fight fires, staying on the switchboard for hours. And I don't know how many fishermen were saved by that lady, between her and the lighthouse-keeper. They were the greatest team, directing rescue crews."

A few years later, the Island telephone company equipped all veterinary vehicles with two-way radios. They were a real godsend, because they allowed us to keep in constant contact with the home office, and meant that acute cases, such as colic and calving, could be attended to quickly.

One day after we started using the two-way radios, Connie was talking on the phone to a farmer when I happened to be driving past his gate. I walked into the kitchen seconds later. "Where the devil did you come from?" the shocked farmer blurted. "How did you know I wanted you?" "Ah, it's the miracle technology of the Sixties," I told him.

The two-way radios did make life easier for veterinarians and their office staff. But they lacked the human touch of the days when the ladies from "Central" were part of our practice. They went out of their way to help people in need of assistance. Whether it was a case of fire, accident, illness — or just a need for a babysitter — all you had to do was call Central.

# 21

## Walter and the Ruptured Pig

I was filling the car with gasoline at the service station one February afternoon when Walter Burdett, a farmer from the Dundas area, approached me and asked about his ruptured pig. Rupture in the swine family is a common genetic condition, usually passed along the male line. These hernias can occur on the stomach or umbilical area, but are more commonly found in the scrotal or posterior region.

Walter wondered whether I would operate if he brought his pig to the clinic. I told him I'd be glad to fix the hernia, but he would have to call first, to make sure that I was at the clinic, and not on the road. He would have to have the repair done if he wanted to sell the pig, and it needed to be done soon, before the hernia got too big.

"Don't worry, Doc," he said, "I'll be over some day before you're up."

"Now, Walter," I said, "be sure to call first." I knew he wouldn't, though, because he hated to use the phone.

Walter didn't phone, and he didn't show up at the clinic. Shortly after our conversation, a northeaster visited King's County, bringing snow and heavy drifting. On most Island roads, snowplows were able to open only single lanes, and the Seven Mile Road to Dundas was hit especially hard. It took a couple of days to punch a track through the massive snowbanks that were heaped like haystacks on the road. When the snowplows finally

John was not convinced. "I can't believe there's a problem with my cows' udders."

I knew this case wasn't going to be easy. "I'm going to take milk from each of the quarters, John. Would you send one of the boys into the house for a bucket of warm water? We're going to wash all the udders with this disinfectant."

"There's no need to wash the cows down," John insisted. "They're clean as whistles."

"I know they look clean, but we have to kill all the germs on the udders to get a clean sample, John."

After some further argument, the two sons began to wash the udders with the Hibitaine dairy solution. I reminded John that this would be standard procedure when he started using the new milking machine. "All the teats have to be dipped in a solution to stop any infection going to the next animal."

John was surprised. "You mean to say that we have to wash the cows off before we milk when the new machine comes?"

"Yes, the whole procedure will be explained to you when the company installs the machine."

"My God, I'll have to think about it!"

I knew that I had made little progress in this discussion, and I knew that it would take another round of arguments to convince John that he had a mastitis problem.

But when the lab results came back to my office, there was no doubt: more than half the herd had varying degrees of infection. That called for a serious look at the MacDonalds' milking methods.

I drove back to the farm. As we sat around the kitchen table with a hot cup of tea, I asked John and his sons exactly how they went about milking.

Finally, one of the boys confessed what he did when he had to milk by himself. "I always put four straws up the teats," he said. "You can't expect me to milk all those cows by myself, do you? Dad, I've seen you use a siphon lots of times, especially the ones with blocked teats."

That ended the suspense. I outlined a treatment plan and impressed upon the boys the danger of placing foreign milking gadgets into an udder.

It took a long time for the MacDonalds to get back to producing good milk. The mistake cost the farm a lot of money — not only for treatment, but also because of lost milk sales. In addition, many cows had to be culled because of extensive udder damage. But the MacDonald boys had been honest enough to tell the truth, and they had finally learned a costly lesson, one that their father had unsuccessfully tried to impress on them: when you milk a cow, don't be in too much of a hurry.

# 23

## Mary's Little Lambs

Horace and Mary Rourke, an elderly brother and sister, were long-time farmers who raised Hereford cattle and Oxford sheep in Brudenell, just outside Montague. I had never done much work on their farm, because they were expert at raising healthy lambs and calves for the local market. One cold spring day, however, Horace called, sounding worried. "You had better come down to our place and have a look at these lambs," he said. "Two of them can't make their feet, and Mary's feeding them with a bottle because they can't get up to suck the mother."

When I arrived at the farm a few minutes later, Horace and I went to see the sick lambs. The sheep were at the far end of the barn by themselves, warm and snug in their woollen coats, which would be sheared off when the spring weather warmed up a bit. The lambs were about three months old, but two were unable to stand.

Aside from that, the lambs looked perfectly normal — except for one thing. Each was wearing a knitted woollen vest.

"Why do you have these young lads all dressed up, Horace?" I asked.

"We always kept the young lambs covered up," he replied, "because Mary thinks they will catch pneumonia if we don't."

When I examined the lambs, I found they had a normal temperature, and the heart and lungs sounded perfect to me. What I concluded was that the lambs were suffering from white muscle disease, otherwise known as stiff lambs disease, caused by a deficiency of vitamin E and a trace element, selenium.

"This disease can be fatal if it's not treated," I told Horace. "Your lambs are better than average, in terms of growth, and strangely that makes them the most susceptible to this disease."

"Please don't tell Mary that the lambs might die," he begged, "or she might have a heart attack! She's over eighty, you know."

We injected all the lambs with a vitamin and mineral preparation, and I left some pills as a follow-up. "Now, Horace, let's go and talk with Mary," I said. "I want to assure her that the lambs will recover."

In the kitchen, we found not only Mary but also about a dozen young lambs, all sporting nice tight vests. Mary was feeding one lamb at a time with a bottle containing milk and a splash of molasses. I remembered that on our own farm, the ewe mothers sometimes had milk in only one quarter of the udder, and when there were twins or triplets, we had to bottle-feed the extra lambs with milk and molasses.

"If you want to save your lambs, they have to be kept warm and fed with lots of my special formula," Mary said. "Will you have a look at the twins covered up on the oven door? They were born about two weeks early, wouldn't you say, Horace?"

Mary looked down at the two little forms on the oven door and then looked anxiously at me, hoping for a favourable opinion.

"Mary, with your expert nursing, I have a feeling that these two little critters will make it," I said. "I am going to give them some vitamins with my needle, because they need something extra."

Horace and I never did tell Mary about events in the

barn. We figured she had enough worries, caring for the large family that was sharing her kitchen.

When I left the farm that day, Mary was smiling, and so was I. For one thing, I was glad I had been able to help rescue the sick lambs. And I had picked up some tips in animal care that I would be able to pass on to other sheep farmers. Knitting clothes for lambs and feeding them by hand in the kitchen seemed like a lot of work — but it was a method that could help save many a newborn during a cold, damp Island spring.

# 24

# Vet Company

A few weeks after opening our new clinic in Montague, I heard that a lot of musical people lived in the town and surrounding area. This was good news. I had been raised in a large family that loved to sing and play a variety of instruments. Almost every evening after the cows were milked and the barn chores done, we would gather around the piano and have a sing-along. So I was delighted when Connie and I were invited for a musical evening at the home of some of our new Montague friends.

Our hosts were Ralph Beck and his wife, Annabelle, also known as Flea. Ralph operated a monument business with other family members; Flea was a gifted piano player. Doug Coffin, a service-station operator, was also from a musical family, and his wife, Helen, was a good singer. Arnold Wightman, an accountant, played the spoons; his wife, Diz, had the most beautiful soprano voice in the county.

This party was also my introduction to Jimmy Cudmore, who ran the local feed mill, and his hairdresser spouse, Evelyn. Jimmy was the clown. He could do standing floor flops, walk on his hands, do flips, and so on. Upon meeting me, he performed his favourite trick — reaching for a handshake and then instantly falling to the floor, landing on his hands like a gymnast.

Being a single-practice veterinarian, I was on call twenty-four hours a day, seven days a week, so I was not at all surprised when the phone rang at about 10 p.m., in the middle of a rousing sing-song. John MacDonald had a horse suffering from colic. "I'll be there in ten minutes," I told him on the phone. "Try to keep her on her feet until I get there." It was only a short run to Cardigan, a beautiful village with a shipbuilding heritage.

"Can we go with you on the sick call?" Ralph asked. "Sure," I said. "Hop in!" I was a bit surprised that so many people wanted to see a sick horse, but I was glad for company on a Sunday evening.

As we approached John's well-kept property on a hill, near a little white church, I could see the dim glow of lantern lights in the barn. Rural homes were just being wired for electricity, and this farm apparently was still on the waiting list.

I walked into the stable with my entourage in tow. John seemed a little shocked. "I'd like you to meet some friends of mine, John," I said. "My accountant, Mr. Wightman; my promoter, Mr. Cudmore; my mechanic, Mr. Coffin; and my banker, Mr. Murray."

Forgetting for the moment about the horse, who was by then suffering from severe cramps, John asked, "How much is this going to cost me?" By the look he gave me, I knew he figured he might lose not only his horse, but his shirt.

"Don't you worry, John," I said. "I made a deal with these gentlemen, and actually they are very reasonable people. Now let's get to work on this animal, and we'll worry about the fee later."

Holding the mare by the halter, I injected pain medication into the jugular vein, giving her almost instant relief from the pain of a bowel impaction. Then I turned to Doug Coffin. "Would you pump that oil for me, Mr. Coffin?" The stomach tube went easily into the nasal passage and esophagus, and Doug had the mixture — an ounce of turpentine, to stop fermentation, in a gallon of mineral oil — pumped in no time. Instructing John to exercise the mare for a couple of hours, I gathered up the vet kit and equipment and left for the car.

John came running from the barn. "Wait!" he said. "What do I owe you? I know I don't have enough money to pay all of you." I replied, "How about fifteen dollars?"

As I drove off with my crew, I left a very satisfied client behind. "I was expecting to pay fifty or sixty dollars for all your crew," he said with a grin.

"That's all right, John," I said. "These guys come cheap. I'll settle with them."

Waving good-bye to our client, the crew piled into my car and headed back to Montague and our musical jam session. Within minutes, we had picked up from where we left off, and the music rang through the house once again. But we still kept one ear cocked for the phone and another mission for me and my new vet company.

# 25

## Doll's Encounter with a Combine

It was a beautiful day in August, a special time of year on the Island. The growing season had ended for another year, and the mixed grain and barley waving in the wind under a blue sky on this sunny afternoon was a sight to behold. I had just received a farm call to examine a lame Clydesdale mare, the chief workhorse on the George Mair farm near Georgetown. When I arrived at the farm home, George's wife, Doris, told me that her husband had just left for the "shore" field, about a half-mile down the road. Sure enough, there was Doll, tied to the back of a pull-type harvester or combine.

George and I walked up to the patient. "This is the sore foot I was telling you about," he said. "She has been lame on and off for about a year."

It wasn't hard to see the problem. The mare had a bony tumour that had grown completely across the fetlock or ankle bone. The enlarged area made walking very difficult and explained her on-and-off ability to function. Bone tumours are quite common in horses, especially as the animal ages.

"She was faithful, never giving in to her handicap," George said, with tears in his eyes. "I'll likely have to get you to come down sometime and put her to sleep, but I haven't got the courage to do it now."

A faithful workhorse on a farm was like one of the family. Through the years, in the fields or on the road, in winter and summer, Doll was always ready to do her share. This was a bad time for George. He knew that little could be done for her.

But that day, the crop still had to be harvested. Jack, one of the Mair boys, decided to get on with it. Forgetting that Doll was tied to the combine, he started the big machine, taking my patient along, too.

"Whoa! Whoa!" everyone shouted, trying to get driver Jack's attention. With the noise of the machinery, he couldn't hear our shouts, and drove on, with straw blowing all over Doll and everyone in the vicinity.

Suddenly Doll decided she had had enough. She put on her brakes, pulled off her bridle, and broke the reins.

The field crew that was assisting the Mair family with the harvest flew into action to catch the mare. But if there is anything worse than trying to control a reinless horse, I can't imagine what it would be. One of the young, inexperienced hired men tried to catch Doll and get her under control. He quickly realized that one cannot get a bridle on a horse without placing the bit in the mouth first.

"This darn bridle's too small," he stammered. "Get me a larger one!"

George was now back in command. "Get to the barn and get a bigger bridle!" he ordered the young man. "Run! Fast!" The hired man raced off towards the barn.

"That will teach him a thing or two," George mused. "By the time he runs that half-mile, he'll be a lot smarter!"

George walked toward Doll, bridle in hand. Doll was glad to see her old friend and quickly accepted the bit in her mouth. George spliced the reins and shouted, "Let's go home and have a drink of tea!" Meanwhile, Jack was finishing up the field, completely unaware of the mishap with Doll.

It was about mid-afternoon when we sat around the big kitchen table, drinking tea, eating fresh homemade bread and strawberry jam, and telling stories about Doll.

The news about Doll came as a shock to Doris. She found it hard to believe that, after all these years, the life of a wonderful animal was about to end.

In the barn, Doll was soaked with sweat and shivering, so the boys dried her off with clean straw and towels and put two blankets over her. Soon she was enjoying a big dish of oats and bran. Apparently she had suffered no permanent damage from her adventure with the combine.

But there was no way of curing her lameness. A couple of months later, this beautiful old mare was laid to rest near the shore, in one of the fields where she had given such faithful service.

# 26

## Moonshine and Jerseys

One cold October night, Connie took a call in the office from a very upset farmer, and then handed me the phone with a strange look on her face. "He says two of his cows are drunk," she whispered. Connie and I looked at each other for a moment, dumbfounded. Then I took the phone. "Would you remind repeating the problem you say you're having?" I asked. "That's why I'm calling the vet, dammit!" he replied. "You are the vet, ain't ya?" Suppressing a chuckle, and trying to act as professional as possible, I said, "Yes, sir, you have the doctor on the line. Now what is this business about drunk cows?" There was a short silence on the other end of the line, broken only by heavy breathing, and I got the feeling the caller was about to blow his cork in frustration.

"Look here, Doc," he said. "I just went out to round up the cows for milking, and you might not believe this, but two of my best cows were staggering like rubbies on King Street in Charlottetown! I haven't got a clue what's wrong with them. That's why I'm calling you! Will ya come as soon as possible?" The poor fellow was so worked up, I replied, "I'll be down right away. Get them into the barn if possible."

On the drive down, I wondered what on earth the cows could have gotten into. It had to be a poison or toxic substance to cause the symptoms of staggering, but what?

When I arrived at the farm, owner John MacDonald waved me to the cow stable. Inside were two beautiful brown Jerseys who were swaying in their stalls, and obviously having difficulty with their balance. "They were fine when I let them out this morning," the farmer said. "Waddya think the trouble is, Doc?"

A quick examination of one of the cows revealed an overloaded rumen and bloat. "Did these cows get into a grain field?" I asked. "They are very full, and they have a maltish smell on their breath."

I pumped bloat and rumen drugs into the two offenders. "It's getting dark," I said, "and it's too late to look for the source of your trouble. I'll come down first thing in the morning, and we'll have a look at the pasture."

The next morning, both cows were improving. They began to eat some hay, but they also had terrible diarrhea. "Looks like they need a tightener-upper, Doc," the farmer said. "They appear to be on fluid drive." "No, John," I said, "let them get that tank full of mush. They'll be all right. Now let's get on with the search."

After only half an hour of searching the pasture, we tracked down the source of the trouble. There was an opening in the fence, where the cows had pushed over a stake, and their footprints led us to a wooded area nearby. At the edge of the woods was a huge pile of grain mash that the cattle had scattered. "Well, I'll be damned," John said. "Someone had a still here. Moonshiners in my woods! I'm calling the Mounties!"

John and the police had their suspicions as to who the moonshiners were, but charges were never laid because of lack of evidence. The drunk and disorderly Jerseys soon sobered up. And in fifty years of practice, this was my first and last case of "drunk cow disease."

# 27

# That Checkerboard Turn

In the 1950s and 1960s, senior students from the vet colleges assisted Island veterinarians with the heavy workload of the late spring and summer. The students were gifts from heaven. For a single practitioner, getting a night off now and then was a great relief.

The student assigned to me during the summer of 1967 was a big Newfoundlander (transplanted from New York) named Alan Klevorick I don't think there was a person in Corner Brook any stronger or heavier-built than my buddy from the Rock. When Alan first went to college at McGill, he discovered that the football coach had already heard about this prospect, and after a few practices Alan made the first team.

Alan moved in with the Ings family for the summer. Our youngest daughter, Jayne, then three years old, became his best buddy. She went almost everywhere with Alan on calls. Sometimes I used to think that the farmers thought the little gal belonged to him!

As the summer passed, Alan became quite familiar with the Island landscape. We often teased each other about the roads. He would insist that the highways on the Island were the worst he had ever seen.

"Why are they so crooked?" he would ask. "And those right-angle turns with the big checkerboard signs are murder! A driver is on top of the turn before he knows it. Most of the time with absolutely no warning."

Alan Klevorick, Bud's summer veterinary student, 1964

Giving him a hard time, I would say, "Look Alan, the whole trouble with you is that there are no real highways on your island — you travel by boat."

During Centennial celebrations in the summer of 1964, many national meetings were held in Charlottetown. One of them was a convention of the Canadian Veterinary Medical Association, held in Montgomery Hall, then part of Prince of Wales College.

While attending one of those meetings, I left the practice in the large hands of my associate, Alan, who was to look after emergency calls. About nine o'clock that night, a call came in from Guernsey Cove in southern King's County. My good friend Kimball had a cow down with milk fever — a term used for a calcium deficiency in newly freshened cows. (They really do not have a fever, but the veterinary terminology has been associated with the condition for generations.)

My wife, Connie, gave Alan directions to Kimball's farm, and Alan managed to get there in record time. On his return home, he broke all existing records of tardiness because of his entanglement with a right-angle turn in the Cove area. It seemed that Alan decided that, after all the strenuous work, he should light up his pipe, which he had filled with Rosewood tobacco, his favourite brand. The lighted match probably blocked his vision, and he apparently was not prepared for one of the Island's notorious "checkerboard" turns at Guernsey Cove. His car, a new rental vehicle with only 350 miles on the odometer, landed on its hood in a ten-foot-deep ditch.

When I arrived home from Charlottetown, Connie met me at the door. She had just taken a call from a Mr. Nicolle in Guernsey Cove, saying that the young vet had rolled the car at the foot of his driveway. "Is he hurt?" I inquired. Connie didn't think so. I called my head mechanic, Doug Coffin, and in ten minutes we were off in the tow truck heading for the Cove.

When we arrived, Alan's face was as white as a sheet, but he was unhurt. Mr. Nicolle was with him. "Doctor," he said, "I was looking out the window and saw the car coming down, and I said to myself, 'He's going awful fast. I don't think he'll make the turn!' You know, he was the scaredest man I've ever seen. And the smell of gas!"

Talking about his close call later in the evening Alan drawled, "My gawd. There was I with the pipe still in ma bouche, trying to find the door while gasoline leaked in around the back seat!"

The next morning we had to tow the car to Charlottetown. The roof was almost flattened, leaving about six inches of ceiling. Alan was elected to steer the wreck to the garage. We were thankful that the big guy was unhurt, but those "checkerboard" turns always reminded me of Alan and his days on Prince Edward Island.

# Postscript: Changing Times

The decade of the 1960s was the beginning of the end of the kind of veterinary practice I had embarked on. Big changes were taking place in rural Prince Edward Island, and in the veterinary profession in general.

Probably the change that affected me most was an increase in the demand for small-animal care. When I graduated from veterinary college, only three or four of my classmates went directly to a small-animal practice. Some considered that treating cats and dogs and rabbits, instead of horses and cows, was a job for sissies.

But as the years went buy, attitudes toward small animals gradually changed. In the past, most rural families spent any money they had for vet care on livestock, and dogs and cats were treated at home, if at all. Small animals were a tiny part — maybe five per cent — of my practice. In the 1960s, when more women were working outside the home, families had more money to spare, and consequently more dogs and cats saw a veterinarian. At the same time, many small farms were disappearing, and with them the number of cattle, horses, pigs, and sheep needing veterinary attention.

By the mid-1960s, small animals constituted twenty-five to thirty per cent of my practice. I had been treating cats and dogs in a small-animal hospital in the basement of our house, and Connie was getting pretty sick of the noise. So in 1966, I built a new clinic across the road from our house. People started bringing all kinds of creatures to the clinic — cats, dogs, parrots, snakes, turtles, rabbits, canaries, parakeets. Like most other veterinarians of that era, I had to take summer courses to learn some new skills: you didn't learn much about parakeets at Guelph in the early 1950s!

The upside of the increase in small-animal care was that I got to spend more time with my family. I hired a second vet, which meant I no longer had to be on call twenty-four hours a day, seven days a week, and I could actually make a dollar without moving out of the building.

When I did make a farm call, I found the trips less onerous than in my early years of practice. When I started practising, there was hardly a decent road machine in the county. The snowplows, for example, were all underpowered. Nobody had a snow-blower on the farm — tractors were usually put to bed for the winter — so there wasn't a farm lane open for automobile traffic after a snowstorm. In the late 1960s, the government began a big push to improve roads, widening, paving and building up the low spots. Built-up roads meant that the snow could be pushed off the road, instead of being piled up in huge cuttings. More and stronger snowplows were on the road, starting snow removal at the beginning of a storm, rather than waiting until it was all over.

By the 1960s, the "quacks" — local handymen who used to treat sick or injured animals — had all retired or passed on, and veterinarians had established a reputation on the Island as professionals who could be trusted. Our pay went up a little — to a base rate of $4 a call from $3 — and the government initiated a system whereby it would pay half the cost of the time we spent on a farm.

My veterinary career slowed considerably when I went into provincial politics in 1970 and stopped altogether for a time when I was appointed to the provincial cabinet.

By the time I was back in harness, the profession was changing even more dramatically. The Island had acquired its own veterinary college; new procedures and new drugs had made our old, standby remedies museum fixtures; more and more women were entering the profes-

Bud's wife, Connie Mair, 1948

sion; pets were considered to be part of the family, and therefore entitled to a standard of medical care close to that of their human friends.

These days, the cost of calling a vet to look after a sick horse or cow on the farm would astonish most of the clients I serviced in the 1950s. So would the possibility that the veterinarian would be a woman. When I graduated, there were only 5 female students in a class of about 125. By the twenty-first century, women students vastly outnumbered the men. Most veterinarians now are concentrating on small animals. And many former small-animal practices are giant corporations employing veterinarians who specialize in a particular field — just as human physicians do. On the Island these days, there are very few

Bud in Guelph, 1948

farms like the ones I used to visit day and night in the early years of my practice.

Looking back to those early days, I am grateful for the kindness of the snowplow operators who looked out for me, and for my other guardian angels, the rural telephone operators, whose jobs have long been obsolete. In a working lifetime of driving two or three million miles, I never had a road accident, and never had to spend a night away from home.

I look back with gratitude, too, for what I managed to accomplish during my career: easing the pain and misery of sick animals, saving the lives of many animals, putting livestock back into production, and helping improve farmers' incomes.

Bud with family at his 80th birthday party, February 5, 2006
From left: Jeanne, Bud, Connie, Joanne, and Jayne

In the 1950s, the hours were long; the pay was poor; I was always on duty, 24 hours a day, 365 days of the year; and the travelling was often tiresome and sometimes dangerous. And yet … some of my fondest memories are of those daily visits with the friendly, hard-working folks who lived on the Island's many small, mixed farms. In those days, the local veterinarian was like a member of the family. Having been raised on a farm, I felt very much at home in the cozy barns, with the winds howling outside and the peaceful sounds inside of cattle and horses munching on oats and hay. And I spent many a pleasant hour in farm kitchens, feasting on steaming hot tea and bread and cookies right out of the oven, talking over the events of the days, hearing stories about favourite animals and neighbourhood characters.

It was a fine time to be a rural veterinarian. I wouldn't have missed it for the world.

Bud with his 1955 Beetle, September, 2008 (Photo:Jayne Ings)

**B**ud Ings was born in 1926 on his family's farm in Mount Herbert, Prince Edward Island. He was educated at Prince of Wales College in Charlottetown before pursuing his degree in veterinary medicine at the Ontario Veterinary College in Guelph, ON. Upon completion, he returned to PEI and practised in Souris and Montague, and between 1952 and 1959 was the only professional veterinarian in King's County. He was a Liberal member of the legislative assembly in 1970, 1974, and 1978, serving as agricultural minister and later as health minister in the Alex Campbell government. Following his retirement from politics, he resumed his career as a vet and continues to work today. A long-time member of the Queens County Fiddlers, Bud has three daughters and two granddaughters. He lives in Montague with his wife Connie.